PROVERBS ARE THE JOURNEY OF LIFE

DOCTOR FATHER
JOHN A. SHALHOUB
US NAVY RETIRED CHAPLAIN

PROVERBS ARE THE JOURNEY OF LIFE

Copyright © 2000-2003, 2016, 2024 John A. Shalhoub

All rights reserved.

Jacksonville, North Carolina

This book is intended for informational and entertainment purposes only. The content is provided "as is" and reflects the author's personal opinions and interpretations. While every effort has been made to ensure accuracy, the author and publisher make no representations or warranties of any kind, express or implied, regarding the completeness, accuracy, reliability, or suitability of the information contained herein.

The material in this book should not be considered professional advice (legal, financial, medical, or otherwise). Readers are encouraged to consult with qualified professionals before making any decisions based on the content. The author and publisher disclaim any liability for any loss, damage, or inconvenience arising from the use of this book.

No part of this book may be reproduced, distributed, or transmitted in any form or by any means, including photocopying, recording, or other electronic or mechanical methods, without the prior

JOHN A. SHALHOUB

written permission of the author, except in the case of brief quotations embodied in critical reviews and certain other non-commercial uses permitted by copyright law.

PROVERBS ARE THE JOURNEY OF LIFE

Publisher: Crown Book Publisher

1201 Evans Ave, San Francisco, CA 94124 United States

http://crownbookpublisher.com/

ISBN: 978-1-966693-00-0

JOHN A. SHALHOUB

DEDICATION

To,
Voice of God in Our Lives!
To my family and all those who supported
me through the many years!

PROVERBS ARE THE JOURNEY OF LIFE

TABLE OF CONTENTS

Dedication 4

Introduction 2

Chapter One Proverbs are The Journey of Life 4

Everything In Life Has A Purpose! 6

Yes, We Can, Yes, We Can! 11

Who Taught Us? 14

Today Is Every Day We Live Peacefully! 17

Your Attitude Determines Your Altitude 20

Life Engine 23

Chapter Two Books Are The Sources Of Knowledge 25

Proverbs Said And Learned 27

Life Is Hard Work 29

The Challenge Of Life 32

Character Is The Salt Of Good Manners 36

Jealousy Is Worse Than Poison 38

What Is It To Be A Good Man! 41

Our Emotions Serve A Purpose 44

Our Emotions Always Support Our Real Intentions 44

Instructions To Young Sons And Daughters 47

Life Teaches Us What To Do 50

The Words Of Wisdom Are Gold Mine! *** 54

Words Of Inspiration Is Treasure! 56

Common And Popular Proverbs 58
Chapter Three Education Is The Key ForToowledge 61
Tips For Living In Peace 63
The Door Is Open For A Better Future! 72
Lift Your Spirit Up 75
Read That You May Eat! 78
My Best Thoughts On Life 80
Twentyone Proverbs For Living 83
Now I Know My ABC 86
The Seeds Of The Mind 90
Mind Feed, Mouths You Feed 93
Even If We Fall Down, We Will Rise Up Again! 96
Chapter Four The Seeds Of The Mind 98
Cycle Of Life Is The Reality Of Life 100
Family Is The Institution Of Life 104
The Rules Of The House And Daily Work 107
Life Is Common Sense! 109
I Believe In Education 112
Positive Thoughts On Life 115
Bright Outlooks On Life 117
Instructions For Son! 120
To Young Son And Daughter 123
Ignorance And Laziness 126
Ignorance Begets Ignorance 129

PROVERBS ARE THE JOURNEY OF LIFE

Education Is Like A Credit Card 131
Poetry Language Of The Heart.. 135
What Ignorance Can Do To You!... 138
Laziness Is The Way To Poverty.. 140
Wisdom Is A Way Of Life 143
Proverbs Are The Way Of Life To Everyday........................ 145
Proverbs Are Reflections of Life Today................................ 147
Knowledge Is Learning 151
Education Is The Key To Knowledge 153
The Mind Will Excel When We Learn.................................. 155
Aim High In Order To Get There! You Become What You Want To Be! 158
Education Opens The Door For A Better Future! 161
Guidelines For Honorable Living... 165
Let Us Appreciate Fruits Of Life.. 168
Guiding Posts Are A Way Of Life 171
Guiding Posts Are Minarets Of Life....................................... 173
Poetry Is The Language Of The Heart................................... 177
Students Who Fall Asleep 180
Triggers To Improve Life 184
Keys For Doors Of Life.. 187
Common And Popular Sayings 190
Oh My Son 194
Continue On Your Way, Do Not Look Back! 197

Plan Your Life, To Live A Good Life!.................................199
Positive Self Talk Gives You Strength!............................202
Poor Minds, Poor Pockets! 205
Ideal Proverbs Are Resource For Honorable Life 208
To Those Who Have Ears And Eye! 211
Proverbs & Perception Of Life...214
Daily Words Of Inspiration For Living................................217
Words Of Wisdom Are Wisdom 220
Chapter Five Education Is The Key To Success 221
Daily Themes:...224
Honesty And Truth Are Foundation For Good People! 227
Perseverance Produce Patience...232
Character Education Is Like Running Water Of Fertile Land..236
Live Well Every Day 240
Integrity And Peace For Tomorrow......................................248
Character Education Gives You Dignity 253
Character Counts Everyday 257
Respect Is The Heart Of Good Behavior..............................265
We Stand For Good Education And Success 270
Your Education Is Your Guiding Post For A Better Life ...274
Character Builds Your Personality Up!................................278
Chapter Six A, B, C..281
Instruct A Fool, And He Will Mock You!...........................284

PROVERBS ARE THE JOURNEY OF LIFE

Apply Your Skills Of What You Learned! 287

Allow Goodness To Brighten Your Life 290

Answer When Asked A Question... 293

Amend Your Crooked Ways And Be Respectable.............. 296

Do Not Appease A Bully! 299

Act Responsibly In Whatever You Do!............................... 302

Appreciate What You Have Of Blessing............................. 305

Achieve Your Goals With Pride... 308

Alleviate Your Pain And Be Healthy! 311

Approach Life With Vigor With Caution............................ 314

Attend School Faithfully 317

Accept Responsibility With Humility 320

Apologize For Hurting Someone! 323

Always Study In Order To Succeed! 326

Attitude Counts... 329

Stay Focused On Your Work! 332

A Good Person Does Not Harm Others............................... 335

Apply Your Skills In Your Studies....................................... 338

Excellence Is Excellence 340

Always Be Kind And Friendly To Others 343

The Door Is Open For a Better Future! 346

Always Appreciate What You Can Do................................ 349

Administer Your Chores Diligently...................................... 352

ACHIEVE YOUR GOALS FROM A To Z 355

Abc Instructions For A Better Life 358

Admiring Role Models For Good Behavior 361

Attitude And Humility Are Basics For Good Friends. 364

Attention To Details In Your Work 367

Act Right And Feel Right 370

Accept Your Place Of Honor 374

Achieve Your Goals With Pride 377

A Good Citizen Meets His Obligations 380

Amend Your Ways With Good Behavior 383

Activate Your Faith With Honesty! 386

Always Smile And Be Happy! 389

Ask Your Question And Wait For Answer 392

Ask, And You Shall Receive An Answer 395

Answer When Asked And Be RRespectful398

Allow Yourself To Grow With Dignity! 401

Treat All People Fairly 404

Always Have A Positive Attitude 407

Accept Me As I Am! 410

Always Be Polite To Others 413

Chapter Seven Proverbs are The Way of Life 415

Proverbs Are The Way Of Life 416

Good Education Proverbs Are The Map For A Better Life! 418

Chapter Eight: The Various Themes on Behavior and Good Education 436

PROVERBS ARE THE JOURNEY OF LIFE

I Believe In Education, Hard Work, And Achievement 439

Character And Discipline, I Want! 442

Plan Ahead! 445

Encourage Me 448

Help Me See The Way 450

I Will Make It, I Graduate! 453

I Dress Right 455

Respect 458

I Am In Control 461

I Believe In Discipline In My Life 464

I Am A Trustworthy Person 467

Cooperation 470

I Am A Responsible Person 473

I Care, You Care 476

I Share, You Share, We Share 479

Integrity 482

I Am A Good Citizen 485

Today, We Work! 488

This Is Respect 490

Keep Your Promise 493

How To Face Life 496

Now I Know My Alphabet 498

Courage Is What We Need 501

Life Management 504

About The Author: 507

Acknowledgement 511

Books By The Author 514

JOHN A. SHALHOUB

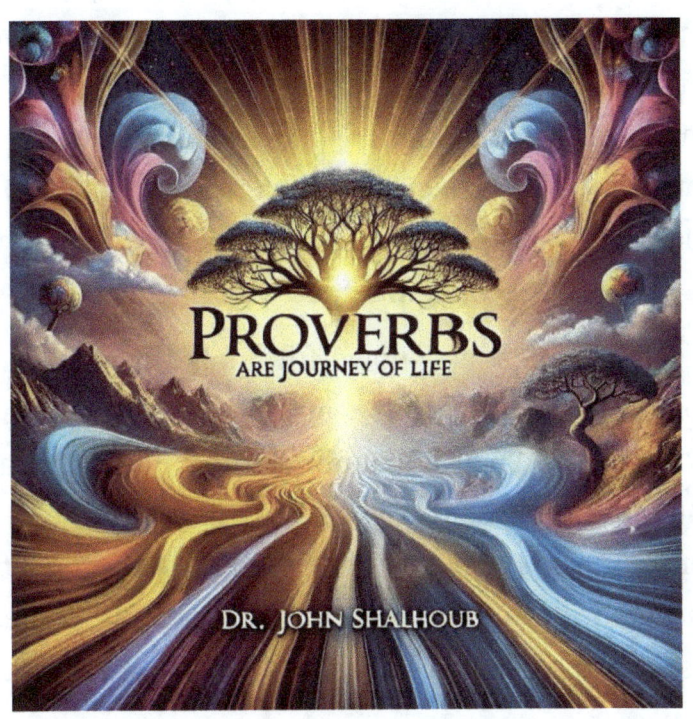

PROVERBS ARE THE JOURNEY OF LIFE

INTRODUCTION

"Proverbs are the journey of life."

Daily proverbs embody qualities that are both innate and learned, guiding us with lessons from home, school, and community. These proverbs serve as the inner force that propels our lives forward with dignity, fairness, and justice. They transcend backgrounds, faiths, disciplines, and nationalities, reflecting universal values. Our character, shaped by these principles, helps us navigate life's changing tides with resilience.

Proverbs are powerful tools for fostering non-violence and peace in schools, homes, and workplaces. They enhance learning environments and promote positive attitudes, discipline, and a sense of achievement. When we invest in character and education, we reduce the need to address disruptive behaviors in schools and communities.

Families play a crucial role in instilling respect, responsibility, discipline, cooperation, sharing, caring, and trust—qualities essential for contributing to society, leading a fulfilling life, and becoming good citizens.

Integrity and honesty are aspirations for both individuals and society. Proverbs and moral values often resonate with children, helping them develop a sense of well-being and responsibility. By incorporating these principles into daily life, we can more effectively manage behavioral and academic challenges, fostering more congenial individuals.

Character education programs enrich students' lives—morally, spiritually, and socially—especially in situations where moral guidance may be lacking at home. This book, *Proverbs and Character Themes* underscores the importance of these educational initiatives. The support and participation of parents are invaluable, and I encourage educators and parents to embrace the motto: *"I care, and I hope you do, too."* We all need to care for one another.

Each section of this book offers insights for every stage of life—at school, at work, and at home—reminding us that character and moral values matter. These are the principles that will make our world a better place to live.

Dr. Fr. John Shalhoub,

Author

CHAPTER ONE
PROVERBS ARE THE JOURNEY OF LIFE

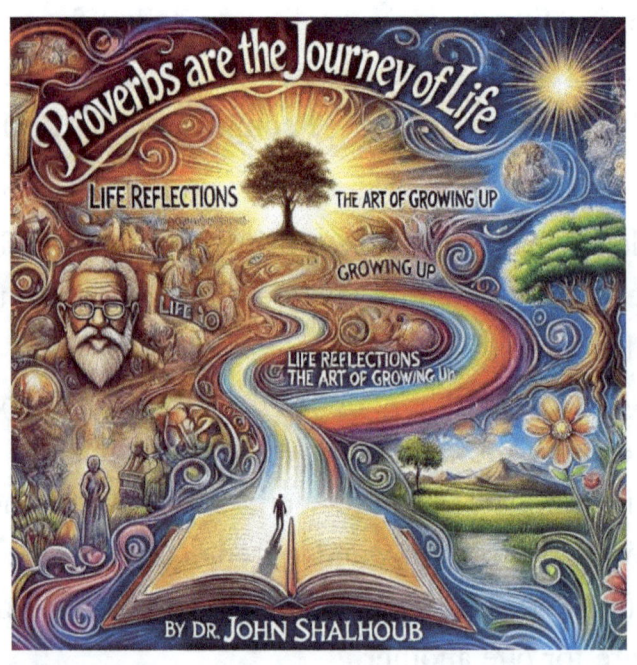

PROVERBS ARE THE JOURNEY OF LIFE

JOHN A. SHALHOUB

EVERYTHING IN LIFE HAS A PURPOSE!

EVERYTHING IN LIFE HAS A PURPOSE!

PROVERBS ARE THE JOURNEY OF LIFE

EVERYTHING IN LIFE HAS A PURPOSE!

15 July 2015

Everything in life has a purpose, beginning and end.

Every problem has a solution.

Whenever you feel bored, take a moment to speak with God.

Every setback is a lesson,
Urging you to try again and succeed.

Every sin calls for repentance and forgiveness.

Every act of charity is an offering to God.

Every crisis holds a path to better days.

JOHN A. SHALHOUB

Each homily reflects personal struggles and challenges.

Such reflections may also help others facing similar issues.

Every prayer draws you closer to God.

Each day is a gift; make the most of it.

Every difficulty should make you wiser and stronger.

*Every hopeless feeling can fuel
Your determination to reach the end.*

Every lie takes you closer to your downfall.

*Truth sets you free, guiding you toward:
A sweet and fruitful life.*

PROVERBS ARE THE JOURNEY OF LIFE

EDUCATION IS THE KEY

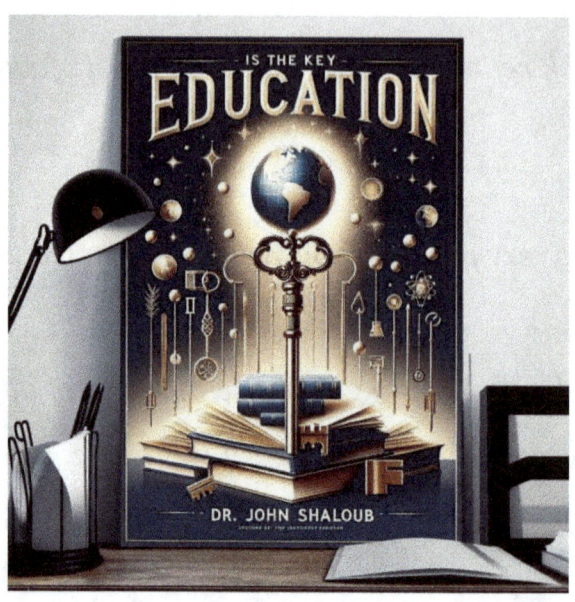

EDUCATION IS THE KEY

JOHN A. SHALHOUB

WHEEL OF KNOWLEDGE

WHEEL OF KNOWLEDGE

PROVERBS ARE THE JOURNEY OF LIFE

YES, WE CAN, YES, WE CAN!

YES, WE CAN, YES, WE CAN!

JOHN A. SHALHOUB

YES, WE CAN, YES, WE CAN!

16 January 2009

Yes, we can climb the mountain. Yes, we can climb the hill.

Yes, we can fly into space.

Yes, we can reach the moon.

Yes, we can walk into class on time.

Yes, we can march on stage to graduate.

Yes, we can sing a song of enthusiasm.

Yes, we can play the tune of hope.

Yes, we can embolden our ambition.

Yes, we can play the drums of courage.

Yes, we can receive the trophy of victory with pride.

Yes, we can chant the hymn of triumph.

Yes, we can spend more time reading our books.

PROVERBS ARE THE JOURNEY OF LIFE

Yes, we can listen and absorb what we learn.
Yes, we can study for our exams.
Yes, we can score high on tests.

Yes, we can embody the spirit of our school.
Yes, we can make it one of the best.
Yes, we can be motivated every day.
Yes, we can achieve our glorious success.

Yes, we can set our goals high.
Yes, we can achieve them with satisfaction.

Yes, we can say the Pledge with spirited patriotism.
Yes, we can stand with our heads high and feel privileged.

Yes, we can make books our playgrounds.
Yes, we can make success our obsession.

JOHN A. SHALHOUB

Yes, we can seek education; yes, we can climb up to the top.

Yes, we can graduate and go to college,
Yes, we can make ambition the driving force of our goals.
Yes, we can achieve our education without capitulation.
Yes, we can enjoy the fruits of our hard work.

PROVERBS ARE THE JOURNEY OF LIFE

WHO TAUGHT US?

8b The Daily News, Saturday, March 22, 1997

Jacksonville, North Carolina

JOHN A. SHALHOUB

WHO TAUGHT US?

30 July 2022

Who taught the birds to fly and the trees upward to grow?

Who replenished the rivers from the ground to flow and the ocean waves to roar and roll?

Who told the sun on the horizon to rise and the earth to bring forth food?

Who advised the mind to create thoughts and the heart to pump out blood and to feel love and joy?

Who informed the galaxies to hang up in space and life to sustain our souls?

Who inspired writers to write stories and musicians to play music?

PROVERBS ARE THE JOURNEY OF LIFE

Who supplied us with the air to breathe in order to live and instructed children to be born into the world?

Who directed the earth to go round and round and the stars in the skies to sparkle and glow?

Who instructed engineers to build bridges and builders to construct schools?

Who instructed teachers to teach and students to seek education and achieve their goals?

Who created man and woman to be families, procreate life, and be the masters of the earth?

You created it all, O Lord, Glory be to You!

JOHN A. SHALHOUB

TODAY IS EVERY DAY WE LIVE PEACEFULLY!

TODAY IS EVERY DAY WE LIVE PEACEFULLY!

PROVERBS ARE THE JOURNEY OF LIFE

TODAY IS EVERY DAY WE LIVE PEACEFULLY!

By

Father John Shalhoub

12 September 2013

1. I will be happy today and every day, for the Lord created this day for me to be happy and grateful in it, for He has blessed me.
2. The Lord gave me my life so that I may share it with my family and friends and be glad and joyful together.
3. The Lord gave me talent and vision and opened the door 4. of creativity for me so that I may be motivated and optimistic.
4. The Lord took my hand lifted me up, and said to me, "Son, I want you to learn skills and sing songs for what God has given you."
5. The Lord said, "I will assign my angels to protect you and to chant glory to God in the highest, on earth peace and goodwill to all the peoples who still know my name."
6. Lord, I will not be sad anymore or anxious, for you have given me faith so I can shine with the stars, day and night, and dispel darkness from my heart.

7. I will not fear terror in the daylight nor in the night, for the Lord has opened His gates of mercy for me and for all those who know and love Him.
8. Lord, be my light, armor, shield and rod in the land of the unfaithful and deliver me from the fierce wolves that roam around me!
9. Lord, be my minaret on the hill and surround me with the power of Your Holy Spirit with love, peace and forgiveness
10. In Jesus Name, I pray, Amen.

PROVERBS ARE THE JOURNEY OF LIFE

YOUR ATTITUDE DETERMINES YOUR ALTITUDE

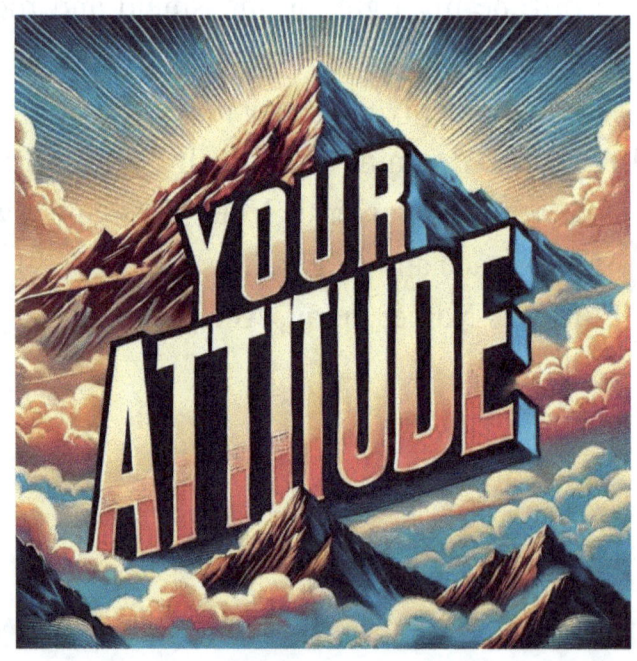

YOUR ATTITUDE DETERMINES YOUR ALTITUDE

JOHN A. SHALHOUB

YOUR ATTITUDE DETERMINES YOUR ALTITUDE

August 15, 1985

1. Bad attitude is the shortest highway, which leads you to the shortest distance to self-destruction.
2. Positive attitude is the highway that leads you to the shortest distance to build yourself and reach a position of glory and honor.
3. Love is the shortest distance between two people who love each other!
4. Hatred is the zero point that will generate anger between two people who hate each other!
5. Bad attitude is the shortest distance to self-destruction!
6. Positive attitude is the highway to glory and honor! 7. Love is the shortest distance between those who love each other.
7. The worst thing in life is to pass judgment blindly.
8. The people who care they serve others lovingly and willingly.

9. Don't turn your back on the one who sacrificed his life for you.
10. There is always hope beyond the hill.
11. and there is hope in better life ahead of us.
12. Life is more that life on earth. It is the infinite mystery of eternity.
13. Don't cause hardship or harm to any one for you shall tend to an accountable for your attitude, action and lack of respect.

JOHN A. SHALHOUB

LIFE ENGINE

LIFE ENGINE

LIFE ENGINE

February 2, 2024

1. Character is the foundation of success.
2. Do not meet ignorance with ignorance, for that is precisely what ignorance seeks: to take control of the situation.
3. Prejudice, bigotry, and foolishness corrode both the mind and the heart.
4. Do not look down on others and avoid arrogance.
5. Those who lie and deceive will eventually drown in the cesspool of their own falsehood and foolishness.
6. The self-righteous, self-worshiping, and insincere will not see the face of God, for He will disown them.
7. Those who deceive others will be deceived in turn, and their days will be few.

JOHN A. SHALHOUB

KNOWLEDGE IS THE WAY OF LIFE

KNOWLEDGE IS THE WAY OF LIFE

CHAPTER TWO
BOOKS ARE THE SOURCES OF KNOWLEDGE

BOOKS ARE YOUR FRIENDS, DON'T ABANDON THEM.

JOHN A. SHALHOUB

PROVERBS SAID AND LEARNED

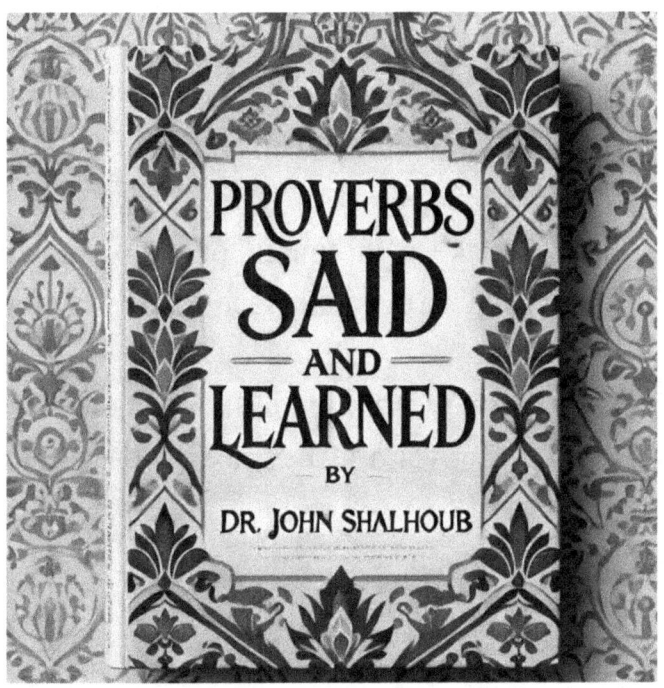

PROVERBS SAID AND LEARNED

PROVERBS SAID AND LEARNED

9 October 2023

1. Don't make an issue out of a tissue but be flexible and kind when you are talking to other people.
2. Don't make a mountain out of a molehill. Accept the truth with face value, do not be stubborn.
3. Don't cry over spilled milk—just clean it up.
4. Don't cry over a lost penny; work to replace it.
5. Don't give up.
6. Be patient, thoughtful, grateful, and steadfast.
7. Don't fear evil; seek justice.
8. Truth speaks, and it always sets you free.
9. Evil holds you hostage to fear and terror, chaining you to the darkness.
10. Have the courage to fight evil and pray about it.
11. Silence isn't what you need; it's the courage to speak the truth.
12. If you don't stand for the truth, you are a coward.
13. Life is the source of your being!

14. Embrace life and be thankful you are alive.
15. Climb the hill and find a way to keep standing without falling.
16. Stormy weather teaches you how to survive.
17. Eternal life is accepting that you are part of the infinite universe

PROVERBS ARE THE JOURNEY OF LIFE

LIFE IS HARD WORK

LIFE IS HARD WORK

LIFE IS HARD WORK
30 SEPTEMBER 2023

1. Learn what you don't know—never say, "I don't want to know."
2. If you don't know something, ask. Knowledge is life's greatest treasure.
3. Don't allow yourself to be a defeatist or carry a negative attitude.
4. Your attitude determines your altitude.
5. Be inquisitive, even if it makes you look foolish.
6. Learn a skill, and don't let yourself end up in the poverty line.
7. Life is a journey of doing work that brings you hope and a sense of achievement.
8. Life will open doors for you. Walk through, even when you're uncertain about what's on the other side.
9. Seek, knock, and ask. (Matthew 7:7-8)
10. Be pleasant, kind, and persistent when communicating with others to achieve your goals.
11. Laziness has no place at the dinner table.
12. Friendship is like gold—the more you have, the better off you'll be.

13. Extend yourself unconditionally to your neighbors; be a good friend even in times of doubt.
14. Don't lie, cheat, or deceive in your interactions with others.
15. The joy of life is in achieving and feeling fulfilled.
16. Walk a tightrope and stay focused—don't look back or sideways. Keep your eyes on the end goal.

JOHN A. SHALHOUB

THE CHALLENGES OF LIFE

THE CHALLENGES OF LIFE

THE CHALLENGE OF LIFE

15 June 1975

01/20/2018

If there were no night, there would be no day; if there were no noise, there would be no silence. Without doubt, there could be no faith, and without despair, there could be no hope. If corruption didn't exist, goodness would lose its value, and if there were no arrogance, appreciation would be taken for granted.

What can we do to live in peace, harmony, and happiness without being trapped by life's paradoxes? We need to understand each other—and ourselves—without judgment or prejudice. We should strive to know our neighbors and build friendships instead of walls.

It's helpful to converse openly, sharing ideas without imposing beliefs. We should free ourselves from hesitation or guilt and resist pressuring others to adopt our faith or values. Everyone deserves the freedom to seek their own answers.

We can guide others with kindness, helping them find their path with patience and respect. It's wise to value the insights of the educated and trained, rather than underestimating their expertise. Decisions should rest on facts, not assumptions or fiction.

We should avoid copying others unless it genuinely benefits us, and instead seek knowledge and experience with gratitude. Life is beautiful when families and friends can sit, work, and talk together with patience and respect. It becomes fulfilling when we uplift one another.

Let us smile—a smile reflects warmth, communicating peace, love, and hope rather than displeasure or anger. Understanding others without judgment enriches our connections.

It's good to ask questions and seek guidance with love and kindness. We shouldn't dismiss others simply for being themselves. It's okay to pray for our spiritual needs, but we shouldn't doubt our prayers or God's willingness to help. Trusting in divine assistance doesn't mean expecting God to do our work for us.

Working together with hospitality and generosity is always the right thing to do. Those we help will remember our kindness. Practicing faith with warmth and sincerity, especially in discussions with loved ones, strengthens bonds.

Let's validate each other, trusting and supporting one another despite occasional negative feelings. Helping those who genuinely seek assistance enriches us all. Let's drink from the nearest well rather than endlessly searching for something else. Graciously accepting even small gestures of courtesy strengthens our connections.

We should help those prone to anger find inner calm, knowing unchecked anger brings harm. Anger itself isn't inherently bad—it can motivate us—but we must remain in control. When anger arises, it should inspire us to solve problems, not hurt others.

Living in peace requires understanding our neighbors and offering compassion. It also demands that we face our own anger, accept our truths, and take responsibility. Confronting emotions honestly helps us move forward.

As responsible citizens, we must embrace accountability, address mistakes, and fulfill obligations. Serving others requires time and effort but makes our decisions wiser and our lives more genuine. Living truthfully, respecting others, and upholding their rights leads to harmony.

Blessed is the person who trusts the wisdom of the heart and the clarity of a sound mind. Blessed is the one who seeks solutions to life's complexities. By working toward society's well-being, we'll become gentler, happier, and create a more peaceful world.

PROVERBS ARE THE JOURNEY OF LIFE

CHARACTER IS THE SALT OF GOOD MANNERS

CHARACTER IS THE SALT OF GOOD MANNERS

CHARACTER IS THE SALT OF GOOD MANNERS

16 August 20

1. Good character is the spring water for green pastures.
2. Thoughts are the ingredient and roadmap for a better life.
3. Good manners and sound thoughts will enrich your minds, and replenish your heart,
4. And make your day healthy, happy and peaceful that we may succeed in life, work, homelife, and the work.

JEALOUSY IS WORSE THAN POISON

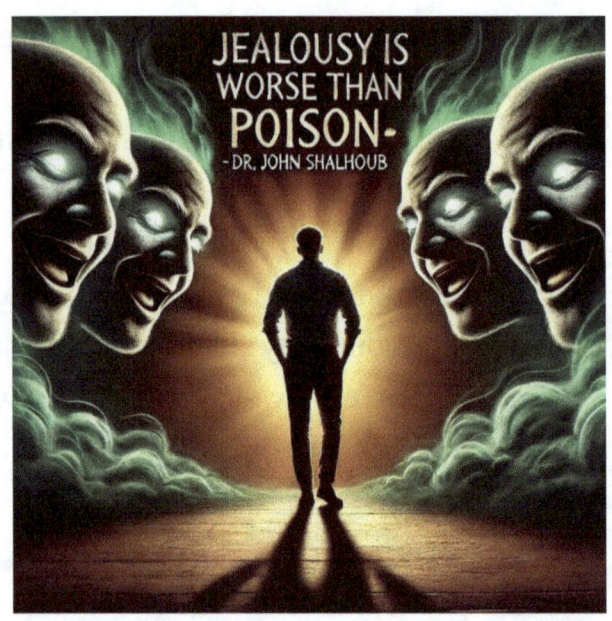

JEALOUSY IS WORSE THAN POISON

JEALOUSY IS WORSE THAN POISON

September 2, 2019

A young couple came to me and asked for some advice about jealousy. Both made it very clear that they are jealous of each other.

I directed them to be seated and to listen to my words of wisdom.

I said to them jealousy is a disease that will corrode the spirit and poison the mind and disrupt any good communication.

Jealousy is the fuel that will light the fire of hatred and trigger anger and turn it into rage and make life a journey of misery and hardship.

Jealousy will turn family life into a series of conflicts and bitter fights where there will be no more peace but bickering and arguing.

Jealousy is the poison that will make life very difficult, where there are no benefits for either partner.

Jealousy will turn the life of husband and wife into a nightmare and escalate until they break-up. Jealousy has severe consequences.

This disease grows in the hearts of many human beings. However, only love can replace jealousy and bring peace and joy to the heart.

Jealousy can reduce the human being into a raging fire of anger, bitterness and hostility.

Now is the time to replace jealousy with goodness, hatred with love and depression with joyfulness.

So, love, peace and joy can make one's life happier and full of everlasting peace.

Only true love can bring harmony to one's heart and will allow people to live in happiness and an everlasting joy.

The couple were grateful and thankful for my words of wisdom. They held hands and walked away with hearts full of appreciation.

JOHN A. SHALHOUB

WHAT IS IT TO BE A GOOD MAN?

68 The Daily News, Saturday, September 23, 1995

WHAT IS IT TO BE A GOOD MAN?

I invited him to sit down and listen. "Young man, there are many qualities of a good person, but truly good people are rare. However, these few bring enough goodness and integrity to keep the balance between good and evil.

Goodness is like the yeast that leavens the dough, ensuring that the world has enough decency to hold back the tide of wrong.

In His wisdom, God granted us the capacity to pursue goodness, honesty, and charity. To be good, we must also embrace gentleness, kindness, and forgiveness, earning each other's trust along the way. It's essential to turn away from anger, intimidation, and prejudice.

Being a good person isn't exclusive to any single religion, culture, or group. Goodness can be found in every faith, culture, and nationality. It's ultimately up to each of us to choose between good and evil. God gave us a mind and the will to make choices based on sound judgment and compassion.

Each of us can be good if we desire it. We must strive against evil, armed with kindness and integrity. While we cannot isolate ourselves from wrongdoing, we can confront it with righteousness and truth. Though evil has power, goodness is stronger. All religious traditions strive for goodness, but for us as Christians, salvation must be our highest priority.

No one can confront the forces of evil alone. Anyone who seeks to be good must rely on God's strength to help them along the way. We must be open to His guidance.

We must all strive for goodness, for it belongs to us all. There are many qualities of a good person, but it doesn't take long for someone to be tainted by evil. A good person must be patient, tolerant, and kind.

An evil person, by contrast, lacks patience and kindness, finding satisfaction only in causing pain and hardship. He makes life treacherous for himself and others, while a good person finds joy in helping others overcome their suffering.

The hallmark of a good person is their willingness to bear not only their burdens but also those of others. They sacrifice their comfort to help those in need. Our world needs more people of good character to counter the destructive forces of evil that are unraveling the fabric of society.

Without accepting the hardships of life, we cannot overcome the forces of evil. We need the power of Christ and His sacrifice to help us prevail."

The young man shook his head and sighed, "What a hard life it is to be a good man!" Then he walked away, pondering my words.

And as he left, I knew he had begun the journey every person must take—the quest for goodness.

JOHN A. SHALHOUB

OUR EMOTIONS SERVE A PURPOSE

OUR EMOTIONS SERVE A PURPOSE

OUR EMOTIONS SERVE A PURPOSE
OUR EMOTIONS ALWAYS SUPPORT OUR REAL INTENTIONS

30 August 2003

1. Our feelings don't just happen to us; we play a role in creating them, often through our beliefs.
2. Sensitive children may try to compel us to treat them as exceptions.
3. Emotions can be used to influence and control behavior, as well as to excuse or protect us from certain actions.
4. We are responsible for our own feelings and behaviors.
5. Competition between siblings can discourage some traits while encouraging the development of others.
6. A child's position within the family influences behavior but does not solely define personality. In the end, each person makes their own choices.
7. Misbehavior often signals discouragement in children. We need to nurture positive emotions and behaviors.

8. Overly involved parents may feel they must do everything for their children, but this approach is often unhelpful.
9. Avoid monitoring a child's every move. "Good" parents risk undermining a child's self-confidence and independence if they don't allow some autonomy.
10. When you shield children from the consequences of their actions, you prevent them from learning valuable lessons.
11. Responsible parents offer children choices and allow them to experience the outcomes of their decisions.
12. Show kindness and respect to your children. Set boundaries firmly while maintaining respect for them.
13. Setting extremely high expectations or emphasizing the need to be the best may discourage a child who feels they cannot meet these standards.
14. Pitying a child can lead them to believe they are incapable.
15. Children may display inadequacy to avoid certain tasks or goals.
16. Helping children become responsible individuals is ultimately in their best interest.

17. Controlling, dominating, overpowering, or pitying a child violates respect for them.

JOHN A. SHALHOUB

INSTRUCTIONS TO YOUNG SONS AND DAUGHTERS

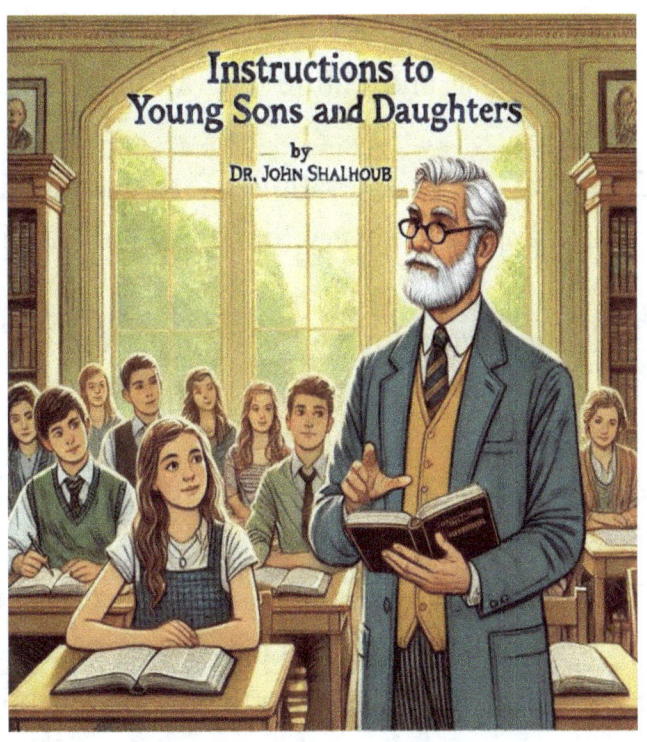

INSTRUCTIONS TO YOUNG SONS AND DAUGHTERS

INSTRUCTIONS TO YOUNG SONS AND DAUGHTERS

21 March 2000

1. My child, live each day as if it were your last; your past and future are all contained in today.
2. Always express gratitude for your blessings and appreciate everything that God has given you.
3. Nurture your joy with love and affection and soothe your frustrations with patience and hope.
4. Avoid jealousy, for it is like acid; it will corrode you from the inside out.
5. Offer a blank check to the Lord, trusting that He will fill it with His blessings.
6. Let God dwell in your heart so that others may see Him through your words and deeds.
7. Speak the truth, allowing your honesty to shine through a beautiful smile.
8. If the world betrays you, do not lose your trust in the Lord; remain faithful and loyal to Him.
9. Love is like a wild horse; when you find it, try to tame it, then set it free. If it returns, it is

meant to be yours. If not, it was never yours to begin with.
10. Do not pretend to be something you are not like a mouse trying to become as big as an ox.
11. Do not claim to know what you do not understand.
12. Knowledge is earned through hard work and humility.
13. Do not lead if you cannot follow, and do not claim to follow if you are unwilling to leave your comfort zone.
14. A pure heart is like gold; even if it falls into the trash, it will continue to shine and never lose its value.
15. Honest people remain honest, even when they are deceived or lied to.
16. Do not mistreat those you love, and never make them feel like they are "leftovers."
17. Those who plot evil will reap evil. "Vengeance is mine," says the Lord

PROVERBS ARE THE JOURNEY OF LIFE

LIFE TEACHES US WHAT TO DO

LIFE TEACHES US WHAT TO DO

LIFE TEACHES US WHAT TO DO

27 November 2021

1. Beware of those who want to walk over your dead body after you feed them, for they believe now they will walk over everybody else.
2. Strangers do not care for the wellbeing of the sheep, but the true shepherd will lay own his life for his sheep, the Lord said.
3. Beware of those who may be sociopaths for they have no feeling of empathy for you, and they have no heart.
4. Beware of the wolves who seek to devour you, and beware of domesticating foxes, for they will devour the chickens that will keep you alive you have for your sustenance.
5. He who seeks to cause harm to others better to hang a millstone around their neck and cover their faces with shame.
6. Do not seek to wear false images, for they will corrode sooner or later, and people will see who you really are.
7. Burying your head in the sand is like an ostrich that hides its head in the sand. So, you

cannot shield your identity for long and the wind of life will reveal who you really are.

8. Do not be a judge over anyone else around you, for they do the same to you.
9. Vanity and arrogance are brother and sister of ignorance.
10. Love is a true heart of honesty and truth, and hatred will wear off like rust.
11. Do not blind yourself to the truth. The truth is like running water of the field, it will water the plants of the field to keep it green and the truth will keep hope alive in all of us.
12. Breeze in the morning, soft sway of dancing trees that will stand upright tall with the majestic cedar trees of Lebanon, and joy for the heart will fill you with the Spirit of God.
13. Do not underestimate humility, for it will fill the heart with joy and kindness.
14. Sadness will bring you tears, laughter will bring you relief from stress, and joy will give you an extension of life full of goodness.
15. Wisdom will guide your vision and direction, and open the door for a new road.
16. Prayer will help you explore your inner life and connect you with your source of life.

17. God of truth will grant you an open door to the truth and will close the door that will take you to the forest where you can't find direction.
18. So, call for your angel and he will walk with you. The Lord assigned him to guard you and hear you when you need him.
19. This life and the next are separated by the word of God. Read your own thoughts and you will see yourself.
20. Do not underestimate the truth within yourself.
21. But if you seek evil, evil will hunt you to commit evil.
22. Be always thankful and grateful and appreciative of every breath you take.
23. The world without God is like an empty drum. You need to fill it with God's love and compassion, and you feel relief from fear and anxiety.

THE WORDS OF WISDOM ARE GOLD MINE!

THE WORDS OF WISDOM ARE GOLD MINE!

JOHN A. SHALHOUB

THE WORDS OF WISDOM ARE GOLD MINE! ***

January 18, 2023

1. The one who speaks wisdom enjoys it as a gift of divine grace and blessing.
2. Whoever partakes in grace is favored by God, who blesses him for sharing grace with others in love and cooperation.
3. He who boasts in arrogance will fall by it.
4. The simplicity of the heart arises from the innocence of the soul.
5. He who speaks truth lives in truth, while he who dwells in anger suffers by it.
6. Tolerance blooms from contentment and brotherly love.
7. Be honest, fair, and optimistic, and seek happiness for those who pursue it.
8. Each of us has a place in this world.
9. Each of us has a role waiting if we strive to fulfill it.

10. Each of us has goals that can be achieved if we do not falter.
11. We complete the works God has appointed for us if we remain steadfast in His love.

JOHN A. SHALHOUB

WORDS OF INSPIRATION IS A TREASURE!

WORDS OF INSPIRATION IS A TREASURE!

WORDS OF INSPIRATION IS TREASURE!

August 2024

1. Never doubt your ability to perform well! You are the fruits of life; be the seeds of the future!
2. Character is your road to honor and integrity!
3. Plan and you will get ahead. The future is in your hands!
4. Good teaching is the ability to be creative, innovative and determined to make a difference in a person's life.
5. Character is the fiber that glues your life to be happy, fulfilled, and content.
6. Education is the willingness to gain knowledge and apply it in a constructive way.
7. Hope, ambition, courage, respect, caring, and sharing.
8. Good character is the map for a better life! Character is the foundation of success!
9. Character is the key to success: Honesty, integrity, responsibility, fairness, loyalty, citizenship, and trustworthiness.

10. These traits and thoughts will enrich your mind and heart to do well every day so that you may succeed in your job, at home, and at work.

PROVERBS ARE THE JOURNEY OF LIFE

COMMON AND POPULAR PROVERBS

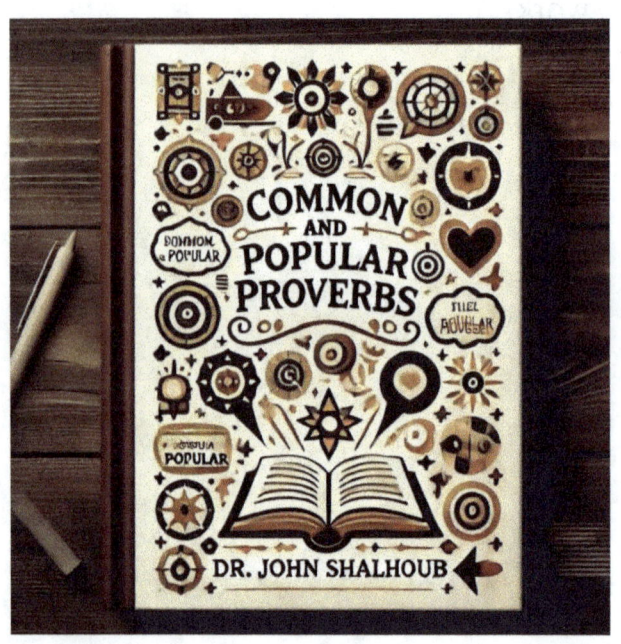

COMMON AND POPULAR PROVERBS

JOHN A. SHALHOUB

COMMON AND POPULAR PROVERBS

11 November 2024

1. You reap what you sow.
2. A man who can drink from a river won't choke on a creek.
3. The straw that breaks the camel's back.
4. Teaching kids in early childhood is like chiseling a permanent plaque in stone.
5. Mold the iron while it's hot to shape it the way you want.
6. When there are no courageous men left, even a rooster will be called a hero.
7. Don't talk about people because there's always someone listening.
8. If an open door is letting cold air into your life, it might be time to close it.
9. Stretch your legs only as far as your carpet reaches.
10. Don't spend what you don't have.
11. A cold and poor man wants to knit sweaters to warm the rich.
12. Moving from under a leaking roof to out in pouring rain.

13. God will say, "My servant, get up, and I will rise with you."
14. As you see me, I will see you.
15. Ignorance is the master of poverty.
16. Beat the water, and it will still be water.
17. If you're okay, I'm okay.
18. Talk less, listen more.
19. Criminals will pay the price sooner or later, even if it takes a while.
20. The wheel of justice grinds slowly.
21. A stone is heaviest in its own place; move it away, and it rolls with ease.
22. If it's going to rain, there will be thunder.
23. Everything has an end—both the good and the bad.
24. The way you are is the kind of leader you will attract.
25. Every goat hangs by its own legs.
26. Every hill has its own valley.
27. When the cow falls, many butchers will appear.
28. Lice attract lice, and poverty breeds more poverty.
29. Talk is cheap.
30. Spilling coffee is a good omen.

31. The one who doesn't listen is like someone speaking in the mill.
32. Follow the liar to his doorstep.
33. God stands by those who are loyal and honest in their faith.
34. Birds of a feather flock together.
35. When you can't get what you want, you say the grapes are sour, like the ones in Aleppo.
36. A
37. An apathetic person is like a murderer attending the funeral of his victim.
38. You won't have a true friend until you've had a squabble.
39. With faith, blessings will last.
40. A person who doesn't know what he's doing is like a camel sinking in mud.

PROVERBS ARE THE JOURNEY OF LIFE

CHAPTER THREE
EDUCATION IS THE KEY TO KNOWLEDGE

EDUCATION IS THE KEY TO KNOWLEDGE

JOHN A. SHALHOUB

TIPS FOR LIVING IN PEACE

TIPS FOR LIVING IN PEACE

TIPS FOR LIVING IN PEACE

24 May 2020

Peace:

God of peace, give us all an opportunity to live together in peace, safety, and well-being where there will be no more wars, civil strife, and hunger but a wonderful and happy life where no one must worry about any danger or fear any terror.

Love:

Lord, allow all peoples of all faith groups to work together to ensure cooperation, safety, and association with one another so that our world will no longer live in fear of diseases, epidemics, and natural disasters.

Hope:

God of our fathers allows us to live with hope in everlasting peace where all weapons will never be used anymore to harm humans, animals, or Mother Nature.

Compassion:

God of compassion spares us from all sickness, pain, and suffering soothes our hurts and aalleviatesour pain.

Forgiveness:

God of forgiveness, forgive our sins and save our souls and lead us to green pastures where humans and animals live next to each other with joyful hearts and songs of peace and the Lord of peace will walk among us and we walk with Him, and His light will glow among us in heaven forever.

Charity:

God of charity, respond to our needs, and provide us with the abundance of Your blessings so that we may always thank You for Your love toward us.

Joy:

Lord of peace, allow us to live in a joyful land where there are no more tears, crying and mourning.

Light:

Lord of light, let Your light shine in all of us so that we may walk in the light of day and not stumble or fall down.

Life:

God in heaven grants us life everlasting full of peace, serenity, and gratefulness.

Healing:

Lord, heal our infirmities aestore our godly image, and make us as white as snow.

Beauty:

God of our beautiful world and splendor of creation, shine over our lives with the sunshine of Your heavenly light.

Piety:

Strengthen us, Lord, to live in piety, peace, and good health. May Your peace will be a gift to those who know You and love You.

Gentleness:

Let us be gentle like lambs and meek like doves and the God of peace will grant us to be kind, loving and caring for one another.

Giving:

Lord, give us Your love so that we may love one another, fill us with your Holy Spirit, and make us gentle, humble, and grateful. We may give one another as you gave us joy, kindness, caring, compassion, and mercy.

Encouragement:

God, grant us from on the Cross to thwart evil and be strong, courageous, and steadfast and not to waiver in fighting evil with love, humility, and grace.

Gratefulness:

Grant us to be thankful and grateful for what you have been giving us: your bounties, forgiveness and understanding.

Tenderness:

Tend to me with your love and compassion, O Lord, and be with me when I need You and standby me when I feel weak and in doubt.

Glory:

God, glorify yourself through us and be our champion in the days of turmoil and strife.

Satisfaction:

Lord, satisfy us with Your bounty make us instruments of good things in this world and keep us away from temptation.

Contentment:

O Lord, teach me to be content, humble, happy and good to others, and not to seek vainglory and revenge to hurt anyone.

Encouragement:

Encourage me to be safe, kind, and understanding when working with others, and guide me in being friendly, receptive, and cordial to them.

Truth:

Teach me to be truthful, honest, and just so that we may have a healthy society, be charitable and respond to the needs of all.

Honesty:

Teach me to be honest, honorable, and willing to be charitable, kind and helpful.

Integrity:

Lord, allow my integrity to be the banner of a shining star in order to produce good and honest work in the service of others.

Humility:

Let my heart be humble, kind, and joyful, and not be drunk with pride and haughtiest.

Fairness:

Enlighten me, O Lord, to be fair, be my guide, shine light, and be my conscience in all I do in relationships with other people regardless of who they are.

Justice:

My eyes weep when I see justice being trodden on by false, deceitful and conniving scammers.

Salvation:

Salvation is the goal of believing in God and all those who should be saved, to be humble, pious, and kind, and to always seek to correct their evil ways.

Support:

Lord, support my virtuous ways, lift me up from the pit of serpents and raise me up into level ground to be a good citizen who would treat others with respect, honest and integrity.

Vision:

Lord God, grant me a clear vision to be enlightened to see the long road ahead of me and to get there with a satisfied heart.

Understanding:

Teach me new ways to solve problems, find solutions and reach good results and acceptable conclusions.

Learning:

I would like to devote my life to education and more education and be scholarly, knowledgeable, skillful, and experienced.

Patience:

Lord, please give me patience and more patience so that I may never fall and cause myself any harm. But grant me love, comfort and compassion and that would give me pleasure to serve the people of God who would want to live in peace.

Perseverance:

Perseverance is what would give my soul the ambition and motivation to continue the hard work to succeed in life.

Protection:

God bless us and protect us in all we do for the wellbeing of humanity and the safety of all those who love all the people of God.

JOHN A. SHALHOUB

THE DOOR IS OPEN FOR A BETTER FUTURE!

THE DOOR IS OPEN FOR A BETTER FUTURE!

THE DOOR IS OPEN FOR A BETTER FUTURE!

BY

REV. JOHN SHALHOUB

1. A good worker always does a good work.
2. Be smart and ambitious, and do not be lazy.
3. Continue the good work and you will reach your goals satisfactorily.
4. Don't take drugs; they are dangerous and bad for you.
5. Earn a good education and you will have a treasure awaiting you.
6. Food is good for you; eat well, and you'll feel well.
7. Get an education and you'll get a good job.
8. Honesty is the best road to the truth.
9. I care for you; I want you to care for me.
10. Justice is to help people to be honest and truthful.
11. Keep your area clean and roaches will stay away from you.
12. Live an honest life, and you'll not have a guilty conscience.
13. Manners teach you to respect people.

14. Never give up the challenge; don't resign to failure.
15. Oppose the bad things that make you unhappy.
16. Peace, peace, peace, we all need peace.
17. Quit playing when you are supposed to be working.
18. Responsible people know that they are accountable for their actions.
19. Share with others your skills and expertise.
20. Talk about your problems and find a solution for them; don't fight.
21. Understand your needs.
22. Verify the facts before jumping to the wrong conclusion.
23. When you hurt someone, be quick to apologize to him or her.
24. X-mas is the birth of forgiveness and salvation.
25. You need to trust yourself.
26. Zealousness is needed when you are a leader.

PROVERBS ARE THE JOURNEY OF LIFE

LIFT YOUR SPIRIT UP

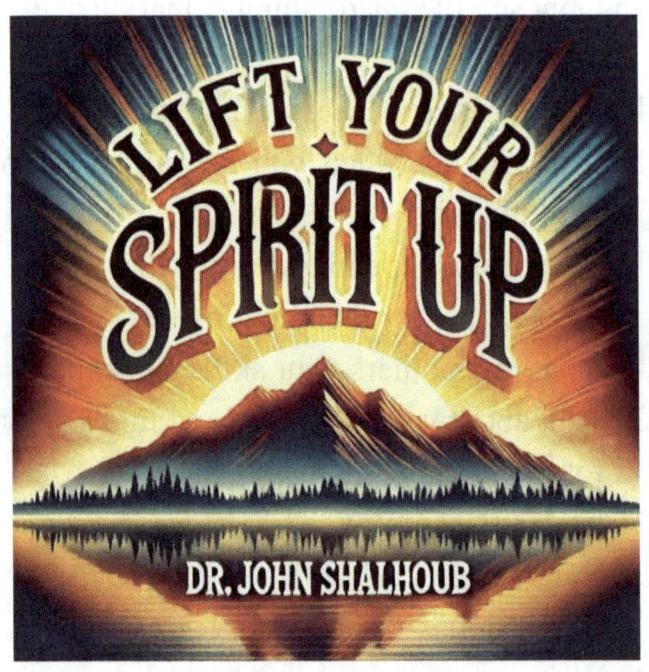

LIFT YOUR SPIRIT UP

LIFT YOUR SPIRIT UP

02 June 2021

1. Pledge to yourself to be strong that nothing else will disturb your peace and joy.
2. Pledge to yourself to be positive and talk about good health, happiness, and prosperity to every person you meet around you.
3. Pledge to yourself to make other people feel that there is always something good about them.
4. Pledge to yourself to look at the glass half full and not half empty, and turn optimism into positivism.
5. Pledge to yourself not to say bad things about anyone, but always have good things to say about people.
6. Pledge to yourself to associate with the best people around you and work to the best of your ability to achieve good results.
7. Pledge to yourself to be appreciative and elated about the success of others as if it were your own.
8. Pledge to yourself to look for the future and not let the past drag you back to the past.

9. Pledge to yourself to interact with good and friendly people.
10. Pledge to yourself to improve yourself so that you will have no time left to criticize anyone.
11. Pledge to yourself not to worry but to control your anger, tame your fear, and avoid trouble.

JOHN A. SHALHOUB

READ THAT YOU MAY EAT!

READ THAT YOU MAY EAT!

READ THAT YOU MAY EAT!

20 August 2005

1. Read and re-read to understand what you read, and when you understand what you read, apply it to the improvement of your life!
2. Re-read and read again. You will succeed.
3. Read that you may eat.
4. Read that you may plant the seed.
5. Read that you may have a bright future you seek.
6. Read that you may get all the things you need.
7. Read that you may learn skills that will make you succeed.
8. Read that you may have a mat under your feet.
9. Read that you may not be a fool who can't read.
10. Read that you may have the wisdom you need.
11. Read that you may be able to lead.
12. Read that you may be able to stay away from weed.
13. Read that you may enjoy the harvest of wheat.

14. Read that you may protect yourself from heat.
15. Read that you may quit fiddling with your beads.
16. Just read all you can read, and you will succeed!

PROVERBS ARE THE JOURNEY OF LIFE

MY BEST THOUGHTS ON LIFE

MY BEST THOUGHTS ON LIFE

JOHN A. SHALHOUB

MY BEST THOUGHTS ON LIFE

January 7, 1992

1. Laziness gives you poverty and ugliness loneliness.
2. Smile at the world and the world will smile at you.
3. The misery of life has no color, and a loaf of bread has no loyalty.
4. Watch the stars. Look beyond the horizon and be free. 5. A nation that destroys its people is destined to be destroyed.
5. Parents! Always know where your children are.
6. Students! Do you always know where your books are?
7. Teachers! Do you know where your students are in class?
8. Politicians! Do you know where your constituents are in your area?
9. Do not buy a coat then check its quality. Check the coat first before you buy it.
10. If the heat is too high in the kitchen, you need to lower the thermostat.

PROVERBS ARE THE JOURNEY OF LIFE

11. Education frees you, and ignorance connects you to chains.
12. Time is as precious as the breath of air you breathe and the water you drink. Use it wisely and you will triumph in the end.
13. Education gives your eyes vision and ignorance leaves you blind.
14. Find peace and you will live in peace. Look for war and in war, you will die.
15. Hard work conquers everything, and laziness doesn't help you succeed in anything.
16. Deception, pride, and vanity are self-destructive; be honest and honest.
17. Be positive and you will feel good everywhere!
18. Don't grow like weeds; work like honeybees and bloom like flowers.
19. Children, education is your path to success; you are the future of the world.
20. Do not abuse your life. With education, you will be the masters of your destiny.
21. My children, I cannot do for you that you can do for yourselves.
22. The fruits of victory are sweet when you love what you do and do what you love.

23. Peace triumphs when there is no more prejudice and no more violence among nations.
24. Science offers a key to two doors: one to success and another to defeat, but the choice is yours.
25. Education for the mind is like food for the body.
26. Don't be disrespectful to anyone. If you do, you will be disrespectful to yourself.

PROVERBS ARE THE JOURNEY OF LIFE

TWENTYONE PROVERBS FOR LIVING

TWENTYONE PROVERBS FOR LIVING

JOHN A. SHALHOUB

TWENTY-ONE PROVERBS FOR LIVING
1 AUGUST 2021

1. If you are content, your life will be more joyful.
2. Find ways to relax, even amidst your challenges.
3. Stand up for the truth; it will set you free.
4. Pray, and the impossible may become possible.
5. Choose friends you can trust and who support you.
6. Do not seek perfection in life; it does not exist.
7. Seek friends who share your values and morals.
8. Family is your anchor; hold on tightly.
9. If you care for others, God will care for you.
10. If you see beauty in others, it reflects your inner beauty.
11. Do not seek beauty in places where evil resides.
12. Do not try to transform an ugly spirit into a beautiful face; it cannot be done.

13. Justice can sometimes be unjust, and the truth is often subjective.
14. Be cautious of those in authority; they may have the option to betray you.
15. Always plan as if you're working for today, for tomorrow is not promised.
16. Never give up, even if you're walking on a tightrope.
17. The power of heaven favors the one who looks up, standing firm on their own two feet.
18. One who plants evil will reap evil, while one who sows love will harvest kindness and God's grace.
19. Do not underestimate God's response to the cries of His children; their pleas reach His holy altar.
20. God never fails His people; His justice will turn their tears into abundant blessings.
21. My God, I pray that You avenge Your enemies, for they cause Your children pain and grief.

JOHN A. SHALHOUB

NOW I KNOW MY ABC

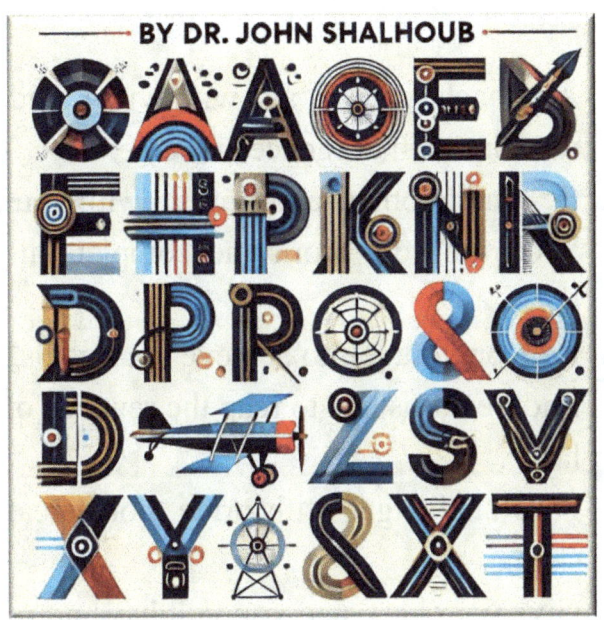

NOW I KNOW MY ABC

NOW I KNOW MY ABC

23 June 1996

1. Approach your goals with vigor and seek wisdom with diligence and care.
2. Be kind to others and truthful with yourself.
3. Focus on your work and complete all your tasks.
4. Rely on yourself to achieve your goals.
5. Endure hardships to reap the rewards of your labor.
6. Face challenges with pride, not defeat with shame.
7. Give your best, and you will have no regrets.
8. Help others in need, expecting nothing in return.
9. Imagine yourself at the top of a hill, inspiring others to look up to you for leadership.
10. Judge no one and overlook no one.
11. Know yourself, and you'll find success even in hopeless moments.
12. Love your family and leave hatred behind.
13. Master a skill, and you will never go hungry; be ignorant, and you may find yourself in line for aid.

14. Navigate life's minefields with care—a single misstep can be costly.
15. Observe Mother Nature and learn from her; she has wisdom and the power to renew herself.
16. Forgive those who harm you, and peace will reside within you.
17. Quit your bad habits, examine your thoughts, and avoid the influence of those who plot harm.
18. Read instructions carefully, follow directions precisely, and listen to your heart in times of doubt.
19. Stop and offer a helping hand to those in need— someday, you may need the same.
20. Teach others what you know, and they will be grateful to you.
21. An ugly spirit can ruin a beautiful soul.
22. Remember, a smile can transform ugliness into beauty.
23. Visit your neighbor and befriend them; a day may come when you need their friendship.
24. Wage war against evil, wear the helmet of righteousness and earn the victory of integrity.

25. Remove temptation from your life and follow goodness each day.
26. You are the master of your destiny and the captain of your life.
27. Focus on your own needs and be humble when fulfilling them.

JOHN A. SHALHOUB

LEARNING A CAREER!

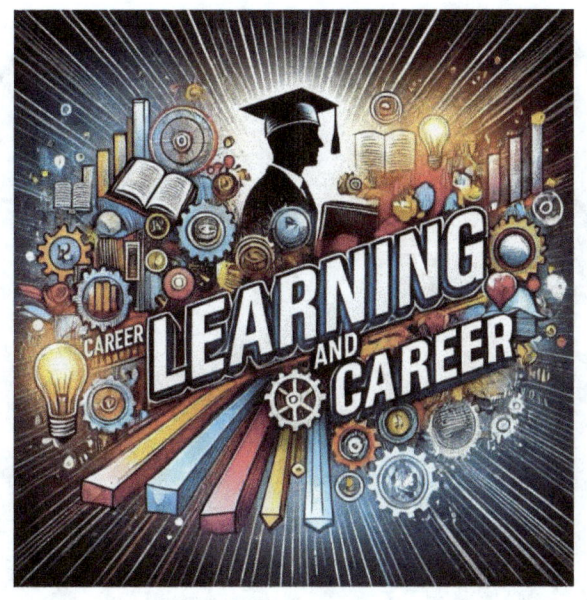

LEARNING A CAREER!

THE SEEDS OF THE MIND

THE SEEDS OF THE MIND

JOHN A. SHALHOUB

THE SEEDS OF THE MIND

20 October 2021

1. The ambitious mind will bloom like a flower!
2. If you don't learn from your mistakes, you will fall flat on your face.
3. He who dances his life away will stand in the beggar's life.
4. Silence is one way to know yourself and to reach beyond your soul.
5. Responsibility, learning, and hard work are the way to success.
6. Children are the future of humanity; teach them well.
7. Tell me who you are associating yourself with and I will tell you who you are.
8. Going to school late is like someone who is going to his wedding ceremony late; he will never know whether his bride will still be there.
9. Be free like a bird and spread the word of good things in your life.
10. When misery visits you, do not open the door for it.
11. Always tell the truth, and you will be a free person.
12. A real loser is the one who surrenders the control of his life to defeatism.
13. Wanted: Students and textbooks to teach. No references are required.
14. Our most valuable riches in life are free, like love and kindness.

PROVERBS ARE THE JOURNEY OF LIFE

15. Drinking and driving are dangerous. Be smart and know your limit.
16. Falling asleep in class will not help you to pass.
17. Learn a skill now, or you will regret it later.
18. Help me! I was caught in my own trap doing the wrong thing.
19. Yours is not to reason why the teacher teaches this and that, but yours is to study and pass.

JOHN A. SHALHOUB

MIND FEED, MOUTHS YOU FEED

MIND FEED, MOUTHS YOU FEED

MIND FEED, MOUTHS YOU FEED

October 20, 2021

1. Set your sights on success and prosperity.
2. Be ambitious and stay focused until you achieve your goals.
3. Stay motivated and keep moving forward toward success.
4. Achieve your goals with pride and satisfaction.
5. Succeed in your efforts to obtain what you desire for your well-being.
6. Take pride in your work and find fulfillment in your achievements.
7. Give 100% in everything you do—no regrets.
8. Education is the willingness to gain knowledge and apply it constructively.
9. Good teaching fosters creativity, innovation, and the determination to make a difference in life.
10. Laziness leads to ignorance; those who sleep through learning achieve nothing but false dreams.
11. Hunger and want to await those who are lazy at the front door!

12. Education is the desire to gain knowledge and apply it meaningfully.
13. True teaching is about being creative, innovative, and determined to impact lives.
14. To be a patriot, you must first be a good citizen.
15. I challenge you to achieve—take this challenge seriously.
16. Achievement is the crown of pride in a job well done.
17. Your friends can either make you or break you. Choose them wisely.
18. The disrespect you give is disrespect you'll receive.
19. Character reflects your inner moral fiber.
20. Obey authority and be polite to them; they keep you safe.
21. Respect all people, without any prejudice.
22. Don't bury your head in the sand—stand up for truth and witness a better world.
23. It's never too late to succeed in life.
24. It's never too late to join the race; It's never too late to win!

EVEN IF WE FALL DOWN, WE WILL RISE UP AGAIN!

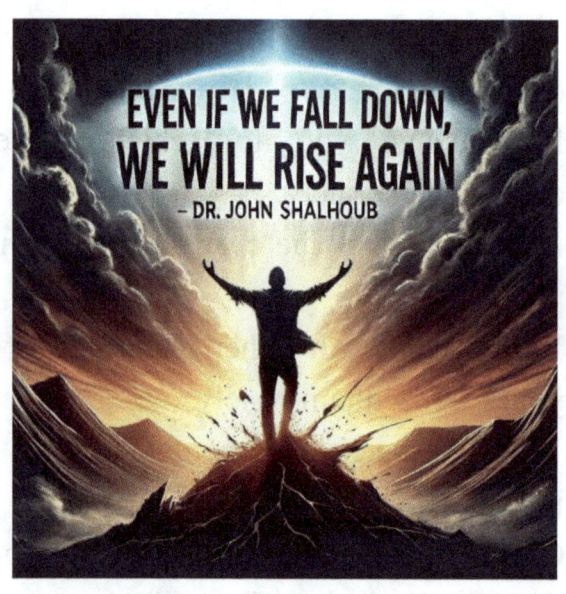

EVEN IF WE FALL DOWN, WE WILL RISE UP AGAIN!

EVEN IF WE FALL DOWN, WE WILL RISE UP AGAIN!

7 January 1975

Even if the soap falls into the trash, it will still clean your dirty hands.

- Even if gold falls into the sewage, it will remain gold, and you still make a ring to wear around your finger.

- Even if a diamond falls into the cesspool, it will remain diamond, and you still can make earrings to wear on your ears and around your neck.

- Even if goodness was abused by criminals and deviant minds, it will remain goodness and shine in the souls of virtuous people.

- Even if righteousness was degraded by falsehood and deception, it will remain righteousness and it will glow in your way of life.

- Even if the truth is abused by pathological liars, it will eventually prevail, and the innocent will be vindicated.

- Even if salvation is not accepted by agnostics, heathens, and atheists, it will remain true for those who believe and are saved.

- Even if storms and hurricanes may damage Mother Nature, Mother Nature will be restored to beauty and a beautiful outlook on life.

- In the end, only what is right will remain, and the truth will prevail, and life will continue.

JOHN A. SHALHOUB

CHAPTER FOUR
THE SEEDS OF THE MIND

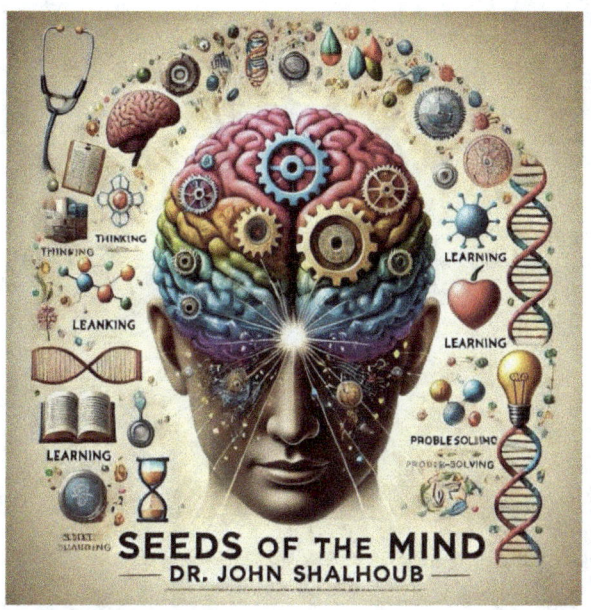

THE SEEDS OF THE MIND

CYCLE OF LIFE IS THE REALITY OF LIFE

CYCLE OF LIFE IS THE REALITY OF LIFE

JOHN A. SHALHOUB

CYCLE OF LIFE IS THE REALITY OF LIFE

9 November 2009

A birth certificate shows you when you were born. A death certificate shows you when you died. Pictures show you how we lived our lives!

- If two people are arguing, it doesn't mean they don't love each other. But if they don't argue, it does not mean they do love each other.

- I believe you don't have to change friends if you don't benefit from them.

- I believe no matter how good friends may be, they may end up hurting you occasionally, but you must forgive them anyway.

- I believe true friendship can continue to grow, even over the longest distance. The same goes for true love.

- I believe you can do something foolish in an instant that may give you heartache for life.

- I believe it will take you a long time to become the person you want to be.

PROVERBS ARE THE JOURNEY OF LIFE

- I believe you should always leave loved ones with loving words. It may be the last time you see them.

- I believe you can keep going long after you think you can't anymore.

- I believe we are responsible for what we do, no matter how we feel.

- I believe either you control your attitude, or it will control you.

- I believe heroes are the people who do what must be done when it needs to be done, regardless of the consequences.

- I believe your best friend is the one with whom you can do anything—or nothing—and still have the best time.

- I believe sometimes, the people you expect to kick you when you're down will be the ones to help you get back up again.

- I believe sometimes, when you're angry, you have the right to be angry, but that doesn't give you the right to be cruel to anyone.

- I believe maturity has more to do with the experiences you've had and what you've learned from them than with how many birthdays you've celebrated.

- I believe it isn't always enough to be forgiven by others; sometimes, you must learn to forgive yourself.

- I believe no matter how badly your heart is broken, the world doesn't stop for your grief.

- I believe our background and circumstances may have influenced who we are, but we are responsible for who we become.

- I believe you shouldn't be so eager to find out someone's secret. It could change your life forever.

- I believe two people can look at the exact same thing and see something totally different.

- I believe your life can be changed in a matter of hours by people who don't even know you.

- I believe even when you think you have no more to give when a friend cries out to you, you will find the strength to help.

- I believe credentials on the wall do not make you a decent human being.

- I believe the people you care about most in life will be taken away from you sooner than you think.
- The happiest people don't necessarily have the best of everything; they just make the most of everything they have.

JOHN A. SHALHOUB

FAMILY IS THE INSTITUTION OF LIFE

FAMILY IS THE INSTITUTION OF LIFE

PROVERBS ARE THE JOURNEY OF LIFE

FAMILY IS THE INSTITUTION OF LIFE

27 September 2008

1. The family is an institution of life on earth; without it, you will not have civilization.
2. Honor your family, respect your teachers, know your friends, and be true to yourself.
3. Stop, think, listen, learn, and grow up and your life will be happier.
4. Learn to spell and you will do well, you will be able to get a good job.
5. If you don't obey, you will pay! There is a consequence for every behavior.
6. Develop sound thinking and see how well you will bloom.
7. Drugs won't help you reach your goals in life; grades do.
8. He who fails to remember the past sips from the cup of doom.
9. Say yes to school, education, and learning and say no to drugs, alcohol, and smoking.
10. Education can take you a long way toward self-fulfillment.

11. A man who does not want to face his problems is like an ostrich that buries its head in the sand.
12. Grades are not given but earned. You must study to graduate and get a job.
13. Your body is what you eat, but your mind is what you learn.
14. Dress up well, look nice, and be proud of yourself.
15. Your child will tell you, "Teach me and don't threaten me." Don't assume that I have the answers.
16. See how hard the bad ones will fall! Why do you have to follow their ways?
17. Good grades are like a bouquet of flowers. They look good and smell good.
18. You gamble with your life when you drink and drive.
19. Trust yourself when all men doubt you. Keep up the good work and be proud of yourself.

PROVERBS ARE THE JOURNEY OF LIFE

THE RULES OF THE HOUSE AND WORK

THE RULES OF THE HOUSE AND WORK

JOHN A. SHALHOUB

THE RULES OF THE HOUSE AND DAILY WORK

15 NOVEMBER 2023

1. If you open the door, close it.
2. If you turn the light on, turn it off.
3. If you move a chair, put it back.
4. If you drop your food, pick them up.
5. If you spill your milk, clean it up.
6. If you wear your jacket, hang it up.
7. If you value your belongings, take care of them.
8. If you break a dish, admit to it and fix it or replace it.
9. If you break a glass, replace it.
10. If a tool belongs to someone else, get permission to use it.
11. If you don't know how to operate a machine, leave it alone.
12. If it's none of your business, leave it alone.
13. If you eat your food, pick up your dishes and clean them on the table.
14. When you wake up, fix your bed.

PROVERBS ARE THE JOURNEY OF LIFE

LIFE IS COMMON SENSE!

LIFE IS COMMON SENSE!

LIFE IS COMMON SENSE!

13 July 2007

1. Life is common sense for those who desire to have common sense.
2. If you do not read, you will not eat, and you will not succeed!
3. Believe in yourself and you will achieve your goals with pride.
4. Life is an experimentation for the good and the bad.
5. If you read like a parrot, you will remain like a parrot.
6. The truth is your best friend and gossip is your nightmare.
7. Hatred will ruin your life, and forgiveness will give you peace of mind!
8. The truth will liberate you and set you free, and deception will shackle your life in knots!
9. God is the ultimate moral authority in this world. The people who purposely harm God's children will be broken like dry clay and scattered like dust.
10. The people who have graceful hearts will live by grace!

11. The people who do evil things will languish in the jaws of death.
12. The people who resort to ignorance will perish in their ignorance!
13. The people who love justice will be liberated by justice.
14. Peace and joy are the companions of those who harm no one.
15. All things will come to an end, the good and the bad.
16. Do not underestimate the power of God's grace and do not be fooled by your own arrogance.
17. God will demand an account from you, and the haughty will not go unpunished!
18. Mercy belongs to those who know mercy.

JOHN A. SHALHOUB

I BELIEVE IN EDUCATION

I BELIEVE IN EDUCATION

I BELIEVE IN EDUCATION

10 December 2023

1. Education sets you free and so is the truth, honesty, and integrity.
2. I believe education will be my moral guide in a world of turmoil and chaos.
3. I believe education will set me free and it will free me from oppression and tyranny.
4. I believe education will make my life much easier, and it will open the door for me to have a respectable career and a good and better home life.
5. I believe Education will open the door for me to treat others with humility, kindness, and respect.
6. I believe education will open the door to self-discipline, organization, and time management.
7. I believe education is the key to self-initiative, cooperation, and patience to do a better job.
8. I believe education is the supporting lever that will help me provide care and share.

9. I believe education will make me a better person and to do my job better than anyone else.
10. I believe education will make me more confident, self-motivated, and successful.
11. I believe education will teach me manners, courtesy, and compassion.
12. I believe education will make me feel good about myself and allow me to apologize, forgive, and make peace.

PROVERBS ARE THE JOURNEY OF LIFE

POSITIVE THOUGHTS ON LIFE

POSITIVE THOUGHTS ON LIFE

JOHN A. SHALHOUB

POSITIVE THOUGHTS ON LIFE

17 December 2023

1. The truth builds character.
2. Peace builds nations.
3. Hard work provides prosperity.
4. Tranquility leads to serenity.
5. Kindness translates into gentleness.
6. Blessings generate spiritual growth.
7. A loving heart develops a joyful spirit.
8. Love will fill you with joy and kindness.
9. Honesty cultivates trust.
10. Faith builds steadfastness.
11. A happy personality attracts more friends.
12. Loyalty is the foundation of commitment.
13. Confidence nurtures self-assurance.
14. Grace energizes the soul.
15. Learning plants the seeds of knowledge.
16. Do not judge if you don't want to be judged.
17. If you do not believe, then you will not seek the hunger to learn.
17. I believe education will help me become trustworthy, honest, and a good citizen.

PROVERBS ARE THE JOURNEY OF LIFE

BRIGHT OUTLOOKS ON LIFE

BRIGHT OUTLOOKS ON LIFE

JOHN A. SHALHOUB

BRIGHT OUTLOOKS ON LIFE

December 17, 2023

1. Psychological, spiritual, and inner self will build your true personality and character.
2. Peace builds nations and people and wars destroy civilizations.
3. Hard work provides prosperity, food and security.
4. Tranquility leads you to serenity and inner comfort.
5. Kindness paves the way for meekness and friendship.
6. Blessing generates spiritual growth and divine grace.
7. A loving heart beats with a cheerful spirit and warm heart.
8. Love fills you with joy, kindness, and a sweet personality.
9. Confidence fuels confidence and confidence gives you self-reliance.
10. Faith builds resilience and humble contact with God.
11. A happy personality makes you more friendly with others.

12. Loyalty is the basis of commitment and true friendship.
13. Faith is the source of patience to withstand the storms.
14. Divine grace energizes the soul and gives self-satisfaction.
15. Don't control anyone if you don't want anyone to control you.
16. Self-confidence inspires courage to do honest work.
17. If you don't believe in God, then you don't believe in being hungry to eat.
18. Every day you look at the sky, you will know that you are alive on earth.
19. Do not doubt God's mercy; know that your right in heaven will not be lost.
20. If you are faithful to God, he will know your thoughts; He will answer your needs if you are not lazy.
21. Do not deceive the wisdom of God with your intelligence. No matter how long it takes, he is true to those who are loyal to Him.
22. No matter how long your right is lost, God will restore to you His way.
23. Wisdom is the source of honesty and honesty is the source of genuine life.

24. My God rules the universe, and His wisdom will last forever.
25. My God, send peace, harmony, and security to man so humanity can live without wars, violence and tyranny.

PROVERBS ARE THE JOURNEY OF LIFE

INSTRUCTIONS FOR SON!

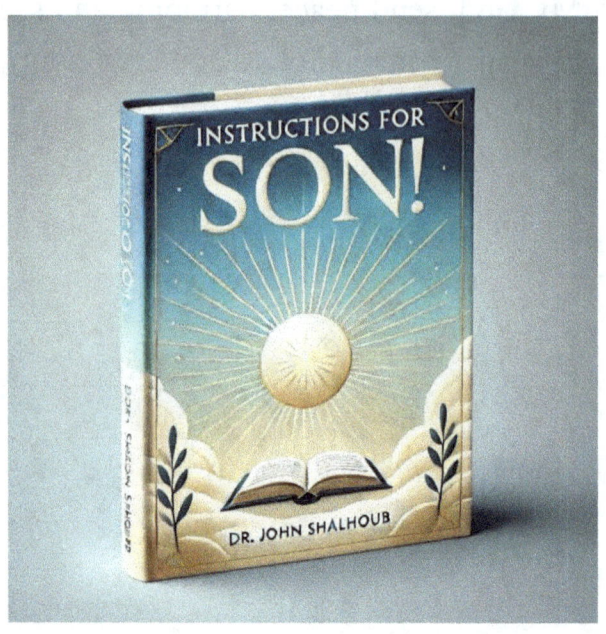

INSTRUCTIONS FOR SON!

JOHN A. SHALHOUB

INSTRUCTIONS FOR SON!

25 October 2004

Addressed to all youth!

1. Son, listen closely to my words and heed the wisdom of my guidance. Steer clear of the fleeting ways of today's youth and focus on building a life of honor and integrity.

2. Be wise, like the ant that works diligently, storing food for the winter. Do not be like the cricket that fritters away its life in idle play.

3. Do not entertain evil or follow the misguided ways of those who have lost sight of hope and purpose.

4. Remember, you are important and intelligent, and the world can be yours when you use your talents wisely.

5. The power of a thoughtful mind and a loving heart will bring you true happiness and fulfillment when devoted to goodness and truth.

PROVERBS ARE THE JOURNEY OF LIFE

6. The excessive abuse of mind and body will not bring meaning to your life, nor will it put food on your table.

7. Avoid late nights, for they will only hasten your days and leave you unhappy. Sleep well, eat well, and keep active.

8. Listen, my son, to the voice of wisdom and follow sound advice. Don't be lured by instant pleasures, for they quickly fade, leaving you with only regret for what you've missed and lost.

9. Be wise and clever. Work hard, study diligently, and succeed; this will give your life depth and fulfillment.

10. The path of this world is treacherous when you ignore the teachings of your father and mother and the counsel of wise teachers.

11. Wake up and savor life's beauty. Take pride in the fruits of your labor. Strive, succeed, and cherish your achievements.

12. Son, the true beauty of life lies in hard work, success, and fulfillment. Those who follow fools become fools; those who seek wisdom gain admiration and respect.

13.   Learn not to surrender to evil, foolishness, or laziness. Those who yield to laziness reap only unhappiness.

PROVERBS ARE THE JOURNEY OF LIFE

TO YOUNG SON AND DAUGHTER

TO YOUNG SON AND DAUGHTER

TO YOUNG SON AND DAUGHTER

26 December 2023

1. My son/daughter, live for today as if it is your last day; all of your past and future are in today.
2. Always express your blessings with appreciation and be grateful for what God gave you.
3. Water your joy with love and affection and your frustration with patience and hope.
4. Do not be jealous because jealousy is like acidity. It will corrode you from the inside out.
5. Sign a blank check and give it to the Lord so that he may reward you with His blessings.
6. Let God live in your heart so that people may see him in your words and deeds.
7. Be truthful in your words so that your honesty may glow with a beautiful smile.
8. If the world betrays you, do not betray your trust in the Lord, but be faithful and loyal to Him.
9. Love is like a wild horse when you find it; try to tame it and let it go; if the horse is meant

to be yours, it will come back, but if not, it means that the horse is not yours.
10. Do not be what you are not; do not be like a mouse that wants to be as big as an ox.
11. Do not claim you know what you do not know. Knowledge is earned with hard work and humility.
12. Don't lead if you can't follow and do not claim you can follow if you don't want to get out of your seat.
13. Purity of the heart is like gold; it is always like gold. Even if it falls in the trash, it will continue to shine and does not lose its value.
14. Honest people are always honest even when they are cheated and lied to.
15. Don't mistreat those whom you love and do not let them feel as if they are" left over."
16. He who plots evil will reap evil. Revenge is mine, said the Lord.

JOHN A. SHALHOUB

IGNORANCE AND LAZINESS

IGNORANCE AND LAZINESS

IGNORANCE AND LAZINESS

By

Father John Shalhoub

11 August 2020

1. Ignorance and laziness are the breeding grounds for troublemakers and beggars.
2. Education and skill-building are the playgrounds of the mind. Play the game well, or don't count yourself in.
3. If you make a fool of yourself, what can you expect from others?
4. Education is your door to success; open it, and you'll find a treasure waiting for you.
5. Fairness, consistency, and persistence are the best tools for instilling discipline in children.
6. Educate and discipline your children so they learn to take responsibility for their actions.
7. It is better to build schools for children than jails for adults.
8. Sound decisions often favor the prepared and skilled mind.
9. We must work hard, be productive, and enjoy the fruits of our labor!
10. Profanity is a curse, while a gentle tongue is sweeter than a breeze.

11. Studying hard, building confidence, trusting others, and being patient are qualities of strong character and discipline.
12. God builds the brain; we build the school, and together, we shape the world.
13. Punishment without good alternatives yields poor results.
14. Don't ask, "How do you feel?" unless you're ready to listen.
15. The secret of success in life isn't doing what you like but liking what you do.

PROVERBS ARE THE JOURNEY OF LIFE

IGNORANCE BEGETS IGNORANCE

IGNORANCE BEGETS IGNORANCE

IGNORANCE BEGETS IGNORANCE

11 August 2020

1. Ignorance begets ignorance and ignorance misery.
2. Poverty begets poverty and poverty hunger.
3. Education begets education and education means good jobs.
4. No tree reached heaven and did not come down.
5. No Nation conquered the world and remained in control.
6. No man deceived lied, and cheated and did not eventually pay the price.
7. Loaf of bread belongs to all; Earth belongs to all.
8. Death belongs to all the living.
9. He who wants to own this earth and Remain living on it needs to raise his hand and tell us the secret.
10. Every action will have a reaction, and every crime has a punishment!
11. The future is the mirror of the past.

PROVERBS ARE THE JOURNEY OF LIFE

EDUCATION IS LIKE A CREDIT CARD

EDUCATION IS LIKE A CREDIT CARD

JOHN A. SHALHOUB

EDUCATION IS LIKE A CREDIT CARD

15 August 2004

1. Education is like a credit card—don't leave school without it!
2. If you're sleeping in class, you're not having a good job.
3. Let your grades shoot up like rockets reaching for the stars, not crashing back to earth.
4. Take advantage of your education—many children don't have the same opportunity.
5. Life is like a locked room; you won't know what's inside until you open the door.
6. Education is your best chance to create a fulfilling life.
7. Failure is one of life's greatest calamities, so work hard to avoid it.
8. Don't waste time trying to make sense of nonsense— think practically.
9. Idleness leads to boredom, so stay busy, and boredom won't find you.
10. A complaining mind is hungry for challenge—feed it with learning.

11. Success comes from hard work, not from whining, moaning, or complaining.
12. If you don't aim to go anywhere, you won't get anywhere.
13. Stagnant water always smells—keep moving forward to avoid stagnation.
14. Let your conscience be your compass and your mind your navigator.
15. Good judgment grows from experience, and experience often comes from mistakes.
16. Overcoming difficulties and earning a C is an achievement; cheating for an A is not.
17. You have only one life—protect it from drugs, alcohol, and destructive habits.
18. Respect is the ultimate measure of pride and honor.
19. Those who wrong others should expect the same in return.
20. Truth always wins, even if it takes a detour.
21. Mischief-makers often end up trapped in their own schemes.
22. Being drug-free is the best way to be!
23. Surrendering to wrongdoing enables it; standing for truth reinforces it.
24. Don't argue—seek to understand and find answers.

25. True education is self-motivation.
26. Don't aspire to be the class clown—aim for more meaningful goals.
27. Never sabotage the well you drink from.
28. One focused student in a classroom is worth more than ten lost in prison.
29. Good people may finish last, but they go further in life.
30. Information without focus is like a door without a key.
31. Education is like a treasure—you must dig deep to retrieve it.
32. Learning should be fueled by a genuine desire to grow, requiring self-motivation, determination, and the will to succeed.

PROVERBS ARE THE JOURNEY OF LIFE

POETRY IS THE LANGUAGE OF THE HEART

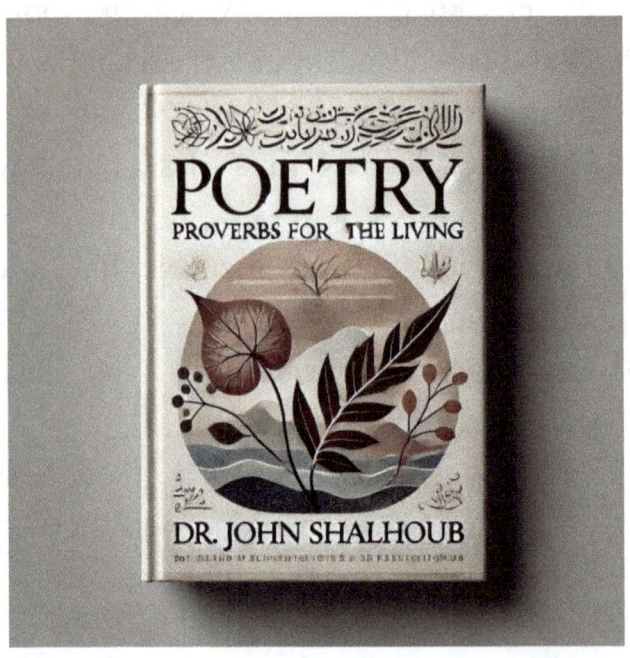

POETRY IS THE LANGUAGE OF THE HEART

POETRY LANGUAGE OF THE HEART

By

Dr. Fr. John A. Shalhoub

21 March 1966

1. Poetry is the language of the heart, and philosophy is the language of the mind.
2. Plan as if you're living forever. Live as if you're going to die today.
3. Do not do bad things that may haunt you forever, but do good things that will earn you respect and recognition.
4. Each person will be judged by how well he/she treats others. Do your best where no one else can do any better.
5. Always finish your tasks; wasted time will never come back.
6. Life gives you many options; do your best to make the right decision.
7. When the Lord is generous to you, be generous to others in the same way.
8. Respect gives you honor; kindness gives you humility

PROVERBS ARE THE JOURNEY OF LIFE

9. Live within your own means and not within the means of others.
10. Treat other people with courtesy and respect even when they're gnashing their teeth at you.
11. Treat people with patience and caring; Do not treat them with vengeance and hatred.
12. Friends are like inflated balloons. Once you puncture them, they're gone!
13. Happiness is as elusive as the mirage of the desert. You think you have it, but you don't. It vanishes before your eyes like smoke.
14. Education, discipline, and a good attitude will take you
15. to the top. But once you get there, remember how you got there.
16. Dreams will continue to be dreams unless you turn them into achievements.
17. When life turns against you, stay out of the way.
18. Do not ask others to do for you that you can do for yourself.
19. Procrastination is like stagnant water. It smells and does not go anywhere.
20. Do not accept mediocrity, for that will keep you at the bottom of the ladder.

21. The people who cause others pain and suffering shall suffer the same 100 times over.

PROVERBS ARE THE JOURNEY OF LIFE

WHAT IGNORANCE CAN DO TO YOU!

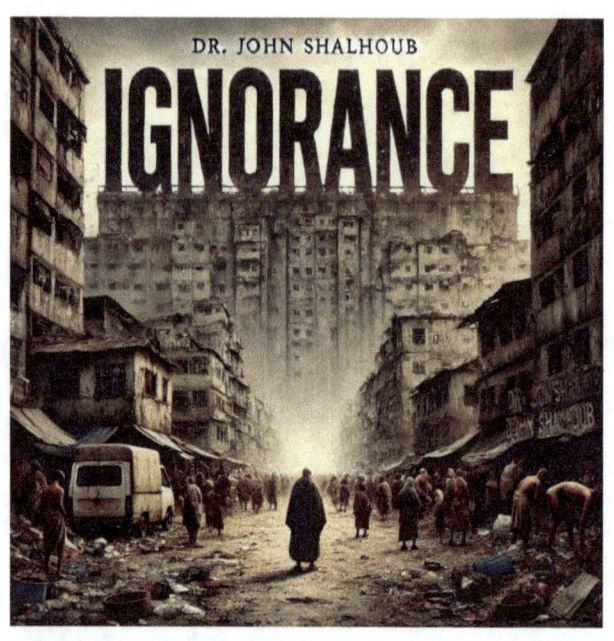

WHAT IGNORANCE CAN DO TO YOU!

JOHN A. SHALHOUB

WHAT IGNORANCE CAN DO TO YOU!

17 November 2009

1.   Ignorance begets ignorance and ignorance misery.
2.   Poverty begets poverty and poverty hunger.
3.   Education begets education and education means good jobs.

PROVERBS ARE THE JOURNEY OF LIFE

LAZINESS IS THE WAY TO POVERTY

LAZINESS IS THE WAY TO POVERTY

JOHN A. SHALHOUB

LAZINESS IS THE WAY TO POVERTY

January 7, 1992

THE BEST OF MY WORLD OF LITERATURE

1. Laziness brings poverty, and ugliness leads to loneliness. 2. Smile at the world, and the world will smile back at you.
2. The misery of life has no color, and a loaf of bread has no loyalty.
3. Watch the stars. Look beyond the horizon and set yourself free.
4. A nation that destroys its people is destined for destruction.
5. Parents! Always know where your children are.
6. Students! Do you always know where your books are?
7. Teachers! Do you know where your students are in class?
8. Politicians! Do you know where your constituents are in your district?
9. Don't buy a coat before checking its quality.
10. Check the coat first, then decide to buy it.

11. If the kitchen gets too hot, lower the thermostat.
12. Education frees you, while ignorance binds you in chains.
13. Time is as precious as the air you breathe and the water you drink.
14. Use it wisely, and you will triumph in the end.
15. Education gives your eyes vision, while ignorance leaves you blind.
16. Find peace, and you will live in peace. Seek war, and in war, you will die.
17. Hard work conquers all, while laziness leads nowhere.
18. Deception, pride, and vanity are self-destructive; be honest and humble.
19. Stay positive, and you'll feel good wherever you go!
20. Don't grow like weeds; work like honeybees and bloom like flowers.
21. Children, education is your path to success—you are the future of the world.
22. Do not waste your life. With education, you'll master your destiny.
23. My children, I cannot do for you that you must do for yourselves.

24. The fruits of victory are sweetest when you love what you do and do what you love.
25. Peace prevails when there is no more prejudice and no more violence between nations.
26. Science offers two paths: one to success, the other to defeat—the choice is yours.
27. Education for the mind is like food for the body.
28. Don't disrespect anyone; if you do, you disrespect yourself.

PROVERBS ARE THE JOURNEY OF LIFE

WISDOM IS A WAY OF LIFE!

WISDOM IS A WAY OF LIFE!

JOHN A. SHALHOUB

WISDOM IS A WAY OF LIFE

20 September 2002

1. As you see me, I will see you.
2. Don't seek evil for your brother falsely because it will get you first.
3. Foolishness is gone and wisdom will come to replace it.
4. Be generous and don't be stingy; God will reward and feed His people.
5. The best talk that has meaning, depth, and thought.
6. Foolishness is Idiocy and lack of vision.
7. Treat others with generosity and the Lord will reward you.
8. What goes east will come back west, and what goes north will come back south.
9. Do not minimize those who serve their God in heaven.
10. Do not trust those who steal your bread and stab you in the back.
11. The Lord will avenge His servants.

PROVERBS ARE THE WAY OF LIFE FOR EVERYDAY

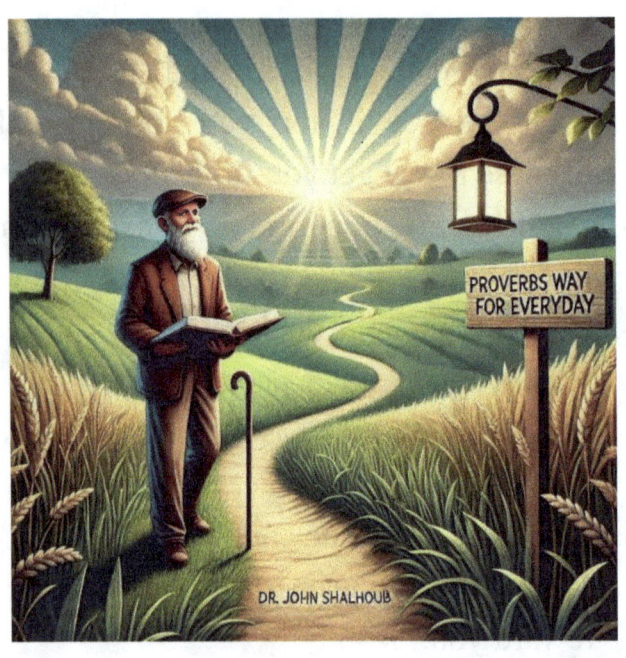

PROVERBS ARE THE WAY OF LIFE FOR EVERYDAY

JOHN A. SHALHOUB

PROVERBS ARE THE WAY OF LIFE TO EVERYDAY

18 September 2008

1. He who bites the dust will be buried in the dust.
2. The one who wins a fight is the one who never gets into one.
3. When you are in conflict, absorb the blows like a sponge or sway away with the reed in the wind.
4. Humanity has achieved technological superiority, but it is lagging in moral responsibility.
5. Motivation without learning is like a wheel without oil.
6. Regardless of how old you are, you are still responsible for your actions.
7. It doesn't matter how old you are; what matters is that you are the one in charge of your destiny.
8. He, who does not recognize loyalty, does not recognize self-respect.
9. Those people who are unhappy with their work without pay are unhappy even with pay.

PROVERBS ARE THE JOURNEY OF LIFE

10. He who steals an egg will also steal a camel.
11. He who does not give up the race is the one who wins at the end.
12. He who can reach the depth of his soul is the one who can speak with God.

JOHN A. SHALHOUB

PROVERBS ARE REFLECTIONS OF TODAY

PROVERBS ARE REFLECTIONS OF TODAY

PROVERBS ARE REFLECTIONS OF LIFE TODAY

Written 7:00 at Starbucks

Parkside NC

4 July 2024

1. What goes around comes around.
2. Some who claim to be servants of God serve only themselves, disregarding the kindness and contributions of others.
3. The Lord said to those who listen to His words, "Do not judge, lest you be judged."
4. The truth will set you free, but you must persevere and be patient. "Vengeance is mine," says the Lord.
5. Those who fail to learn from past mistakes are doomed to repeat them.
6. Those who harm others will fall into their own traps; nothing escapes God's attention.
7. If people would reflect on the harm their actions cause others,
8. they might realize that they cannot escape the consequences of their actions.

9. Arrogance and selfishness cannot justify obnoxious behavior. Undermining others with negativity and destructiveness will only bring harm to oneself.
10. When behavior is not driven by a desire for harmony and peace, it will ultimately end in failure.
11. Godly love should bring people together
12. to share peace, social harmony, and spiritual joy.
13. Parents, love your children and teach them kindness, the joy of life, and the spiritual rewards of a happy family.
14. Home should be a place to learn love, family values, care, sharing and to embrace God's grace as a gift of life.
15. Boys and girls, cherish your home, seek education, respect your parents, and contribute to the well-being of your family, society, and country.
16. Know yourself, be loyal to your heritage, treat others with love and compassion, and remain tolerant, courageous, and cheerful; God's love will blanket you with peace on earth and in heaven.

PROVERBS ARE THE JOURNEY OF LIFE

17. Be fruitful, productive, thankful, and grateful.
18. Do not turn your back on those who have shown you kindness.
19. The sun shines on all, but only those who look up and say, "Thank you, Lord, for the gift of life and the beauty of this day," will truly enjoy God's blessings.
20. It's heartwarming to see young people working in coffee shops, bringing smiles to those who walk in each morning with hope for a brighter day.
21. Life is about seeing beauty in everything around you.
22. Goodness is the joy in your heart when you see a young person being courteous and helpful.
23. The smile of the day is when someone adds joy by opening a door, offering a helping hand, and reminding us of the good in humanity.

JOHN A. SHALHOUB

KNOWLEDGE IS LEARNING

KNOWLEDGE IS LEARNING

PROVERBS ARE THE JOURNEY OF LIFE

KNOWLEDGE IS LEARNING

May 18, 2024

1. Learning is from cradle to grave!
2. Knowledge at a young age is like engraving in a stone.
3. Education is the life jacket in life.
4. Don't underestimate the little ones. Do not make fun of the elderly.
5. Faith is like sleeping in the bosom of comfort; he gives you mercy and reassurance.
6. This life is a journey to whomever he accepts God; He gives existence to its existence.
7. Whoever claims false greatness will fall from his horse to ride on someone else's donkey.
8. No nation trusted a foreigner and I remained steadfast.
9. If you die at the hands of tyrants, you will live in the book of the living in heaven.
10. No matter how long it takes, God will compensate whoever serves Him with honor and integrity.

JOHN A. SHALHOUB

EDUCATION IS THE KEY OF KNOWLEDGE

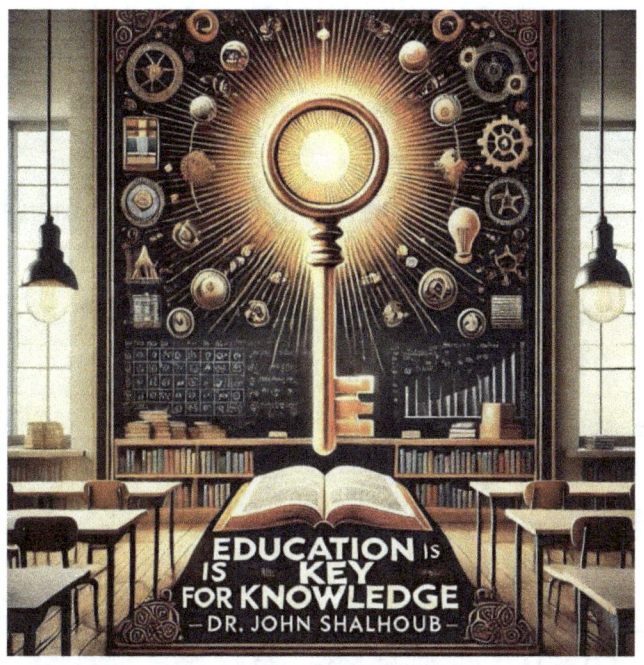

EDUCATION IS THE KEY OF KNOWLEDGE

EDUCATION IS THE KEY OF KNOWLEDGE

09/25/2006

1. If a man treats you just like he treats himself, he is a fair man.
2. A society that does not provide its members with protection, health care, free education and an opportunity to work is destined for failure and disintegration.
3. Education without inspiration is like religion without God.
4. Passion is like makeup. It wears off very quickly.
5. An oilman thinks of oil, but a hungry man thinks of a loaf of bread.
6. Love is like silver; the more you shine it, the brighter it becomes.
7. A nation that lacks inspiration and education will decline into mediocrity.
8. The secret of success in education is to listen to your instructors, work hard, and do what you must do to reach up the hill.

9. Ignorance is laziness; the more you have of it, the lonelier you become.
10. Bigotry is like corrosion; it destroys itself and all that it touches.

PROVERBS ARE THE JOURNEY OF LIFE

THE MIND WILL EXCEL WHEN WE LEARN!

THE MIND WILL EXCEL WHEN WE LEARN!

JOHN A. SHALHOUB

THE MIND WILL EXCEL WHEN WE LEARN

22 October 2021

1. The mind excels when education and books become your friends. Use your potential and skills to become a successful member of society.
2. Alcohol, drugs, and gambling are enemies of the mind and humanity.
3. Education is your lifejacket in this chaotic world, protecting you from poverty and need.
4. Let us speak the truth to be free, for lies make us slaves to evil minds and bigotry.
5. Laziness breeds boredom, and boredom breeds poverty.
6. Never tire of learning new things! Learn from the honeybee that tirelessly creates honey.
7. Great success is achieved when students engage with books, not by wandering the streets.
8. It's not your aptitude but your attitude that determines your altitude.
9. If you do not seek education, poverty will seek you.

PROVERBS ARE THE JOURNEY OF LIFE

10. The price of foolishness today is a reprimand; tomorrow, it might be your life.
11. Don't waste time questioning every rule—focus on doing what's right.
12. Your priority should be learning, graduating, and moving forward in life.
13. It is better to build schools for struggling students than jails for irresponsible adults.
14. Education is the key to rewarding careers and fulfilling jobs.
15. Teachers are the hinges that open doors to knowledge, discipline, and learning.
16. If you don't use your mind, it will grow rusty. Learn a skill, or face hunger.
17. Ignorance, prejudice, and dishonesty make the world an unhappy place.

JOHN A. SHALHOUB

AIM HIGH IN ORDER TO GET THERE!

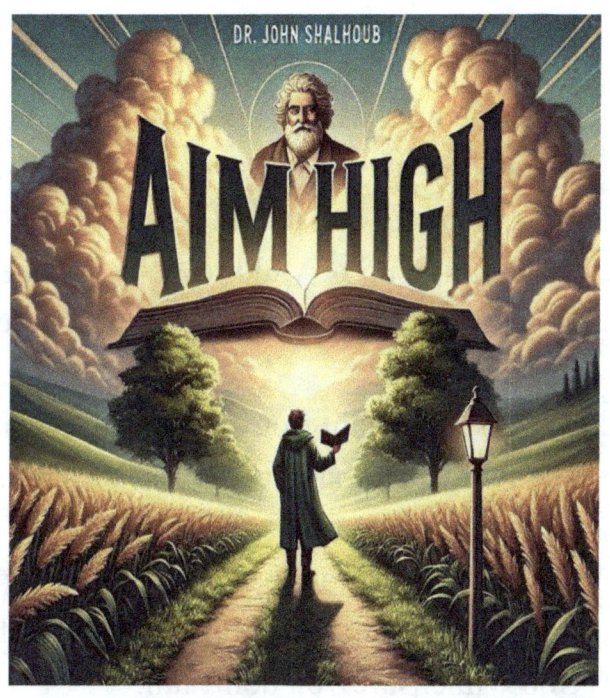

AIM HIGH IN ORDER TO GET THERE!

AIM HIGH IN ORDER TO GET THERE! YOU BECOME WHAT YOU WANT TO BE!

17 July 2024

1. You become what you set your mind to. Achieving your dreams requires hard work, determination, and relentless spirit.
2. Do not give up or yield to defeat. Once you set your hands to the plow, look forward and stay the course.
3. Faith will sustain you through moments of discouragement as the sun rises each day to shine its light.
4. Hope will light your path, faith will keep you steady, perseverance will hold your hand, and God will ensure you don't fall.
5. Each day has its own purpose. Like a farmer, you plant seeds with hope and reap with gratitude. Never give up—not today, not tomorrow.
6. God sees your journey, and life will bring what He allows. Laziness bears no fruit; only effort and dedication can yield success.

7. Start your morning by saying, "Lord, open doors, make today a good day, and help me bring happiness to others."
8. Good character is the foundation of success. Don't reward ignorance nor respond to prejudice, bigotry, or arrogance.
9. Deception and lies only trap those who spread them.
10. The righteous worship God, while the selfish worship themselves—and in doing so, distance themselves from His presence.

EDUCATION OPENS THE DOOR FOR BETTER FUTURE

EDUCATION OPENS THE DOOR FOR BETTER FUTURE

EDUCATION OPENS THE DOOR FOR A BETTER FUTURE!

For all readers

1. A good worker always does a good work.
2. Be smart and ambitious, and do not be lazy.
3. Continue the good work and you will reach your goals satisfactorily.
4. Don't take drugs; they are dangerous and bad for you.
5. Earn a good education and you will have a treasure awaiting you.
6. Food is good for you; eat well, and you'll feel well.
7. Get an education and you'll get a good job.
8. Honesty is the best road to the truth.
9. I care for you; I want you to care for me.
10. Justice is to help people to be honest and truthful.
11. Keep your area clean and roaches will stay away from you.
12. Live an honest life, and you'll not have a guilty conscience.
13. Manners teach you to respect people.
14. Never give up the challenge; don't resign to failure.

15. Oppose the bad things that make you unhappy.
16. Peace, peace, peace, we all need peace.
17. Quit playing when you are supposed to be working.
18. Responsible people know that they are accountable for their actions.
1) Share with others your skills and expertise.
2) Talk about your problems and find a solution for them; don't fight.
3) Understand your needs.
4) Verify the facts before jumping to the wrong conclusion.
5) When you hurt someone, be quick to apologize to him or her.
6) Xmas is the birth of forgiveness and salvation.
7) You need to trust yourself.
8) Zealousness is needed when you are a leader.

CHAPTER FIVE
CHARACTER EDUCATION

Character Education is the fiber that glues your life to be happy, fulfilled, and content.

Learning is gaining knowledge and applying it in a constructive way!

PROVERBS ARE THE JOURNEY OF LIFE

GUIDELINES FOR HONORABLE LIVING

GUIDELINES FOR HONORABLE LIVING

GUIDELINES FOR HONORABLE LIVING

21 March 2004

1. Don't be a worrier. By worrying, you relive the same event repeatedly, causing yourself more anguish.
2. Instead, learn to pray and cultivate positive thoughts.
3. Avoid controlling others for personal gain. Every human being has the right to govern their own life.
4. Do not seek false glory for selfish reasons. Allow God to be glorified in His own creation. Even an atheist will, at some point, need a higher power.
5. Don't be consumed by greed or selfishness. Money is meant to serve our needs without causing harm to others.
6. The love of money can lead to evil when used to harm.
7. Harm no one by word, thought, or deed. Inflicting harm only adds to the world's misery. Learn to forgive.
8. Do not harbor anger. Anger injures the one who feels it. It is like acid: it corrodes

everything around it, including the person holding onto it.
9. Take responsibility for your own actions. Do not blame others for your misfortunes.
10. Make time for leisure. Relaxation reduces stress, worry, and anxiety.
11. Cultivate a sense of humor. A cheerful demeanor and a smile make you less angry and more approachable.
12. Enjoy the beauty of life. Appreciate the good things around you, for God has made life beautiful and wonderful.

JOHN A. SHALHOUB

LET US REMEMBER THE FRUITS OF LIFE

LET US REMEMBER THE FRUITS OF LIFE

LET US APPRECIATE FRUITS OF LIFE

17 September 2024

1. We need to recognize life's signals and acknowledge our struggle to find a place where we can settle, achieve our goals, and live in peace.
2. The irony—and the secret—is to never give up. With perseverance, we will get there.
3. Along the way, we may hit snags or face setbacks. This just means it's time to take a detour or change course.
4. So, we must stay determined, persist, and keep our focus on achieving our goals.
5. No matter how long it takes, we cannot surrender to failure or hopelessness.
6. In the rhythm of daily life, we can't just sit idle. If we do, we risk failure and loss.
7. Sooner or later, there will be light at the end of the tunnel.
8. The door will open, and we will reach our goals.
9. The essence of life is to keep your eyes on the prize. Be resilient, aim high, and stay true. Keep working hard, stay connected to

society, use available resources, and face challenges head-on until you reach your objective.
10. Life is rarely a bed of roses, even for the wealthy. Many have honed skills to invest and use their wealth for societal good, but even they face misfortune. Losing a job, for instance, tests one's perseverance and resilience.
11. A positive attitude, confidence, consistency, and continuous effort will bring steadiness. These qualities energize and motivate, helping you avoid surrendering to weakness or failure.
12. Life requires you to take intelligent risks, explore options, and stay proactive. Laziness brings nothing but regret and disappointment.
13. When life gives you lemons, make lemonade.
14. We may wish for complete control over life, but its mysteries force us to rely on faith, as the future remains unknown.
15. So, we keep moving through the mud until we find our way out.

PROVERBS ARE THE JOURNEY OF LIFE

GUIDING POSTS ARE A WAY OF LIFE

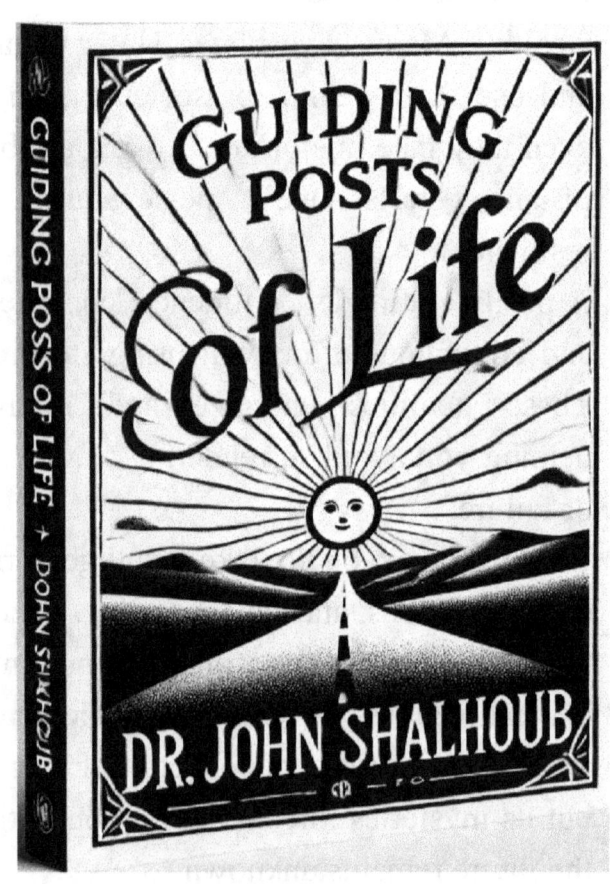

GUIDING POSTS ARE A WAY OF LIFE

GUIDING POSTS ARE A WAY OF LIFE

4 October 2024

1. The most destructive habit in life is **deception**.
2. The worst enemy of success is **laziness**.
3. The nastiest human trait is **betrayal**.
4. The enemy of the mind is **despair**.
5. The deadliest poison is **dishonesty**.
6. The most defeatist attitude is **giving up**.
7. The most awful habit is **gossip**.
8. The ugliest sin is **greed**.
9. The worst social disaster is **corruption**.
10. The most humiliating disgrace is the loss of **honor**.
11. The enemy of the heart is **worry**.
12. The greatest honor is the courage to stand for **truth**.
13. The finest human quality is **tolerance**.
14. The most powerful tool for survival is **perseverance**.
15. The noblest philanthropic act is **giving**.
16. The most effective defense is **honesty**.
17. The greatest joy in life is **family**.
18. The most amazing mystery is **one's life**.
19. The most powerful inner force is **faith**.
20. The most trusted friend is **prayer**.
21. The best communication skill is **listening**.

22. The best personal characteristic is **genuineness**.
23. The friendliest language is **a warm smile**.
24. The most gracious gift of life is **love**.
25. The most helpful healing tool is **comfort**.
26. The most effective vitamin is **encouragement**.
27. The most precious qualities of living are **integrity, truthfulness, and a good reputation**.

JOHN A. SHALHOUB

GUIDING POSTS ARE MINARETS OF LIFE

GUIDING POSTS ARE MINARETS OF LIFE

GUIDING POSTS ARE MINARETS OF LIFE

28 September 2003

1. Education is like a credit card—don't leave school without it!
2. Students who fall asleep in class may find it hard to pass.
3. Let your grades soar like rockets to the stars.
4. Don't let your grades crash like falling rockets.
5. Make the most of your education; many children don't have the same opportunity.
6. Life is like a locked room—you won't know what's inside until you open the door.
7. Education is your best tool to make the most of your life.
8. The greatest calamity in life is failure.
9. Don't waste time making sense of nonsense; think pragmatically.
10. Idleness leads to boredom—stay busy and keep boredom at bay.
11. Whining is the sign of a restless mind; turn it into studying.
12. Whining, moaning, and complaining won't lead to success.

13. Only hard work will.
14. If you don't aim to go anywhere, you won't get anywhere!
15. Stagnant water eventually stinks.
16. Let your conscience be your compass and your mind be your navigator.
17. Good judgment comes from experience, and experience often comes from poor decisions.
18. Overcoming challenges to earn an A, B, or C is an accomplishment; cheating to get an A is not.
19. You have one life to live—protect it from drugs, alcohol, and bad habits.
20. Respect is the ultimate mark of self-worth.
21. Those who harm others should expect harm in return.
22. The truth always prevails, even if it takes a detour.
23. Those who hurt others should be prepared to face the same.
24. Those who scheme will eventually fall into their own traps.
25. Stay drug-free—it's the way to be!
26. Surrendering to evil fuels evil; standing by the truth fuels truth.
27. Don't argue; seek the answers you need.

28. Education is self-motivation.
29. Don't be the class clown; that shouldn't be all you are in life.
30. Don't throw stones at the well you just drank from.
31. One student in the class is better than ten in prison.
32. Good guys may finish last, but they go further in life.
33. Information without focus is like a door without a key.
34. Education is like a credit card—don't leave home without it.
35. The student is his own best teacher; the teacher is just a coach.
36. Education is like a treasure; you must dig deep to retrieve it.
37. Education should be driven by the desire to learn.
38. Education is self-motivation, determination, and the will to succeed.

JOHN A. SHALHOUB

POETRY IS THE LANGUAGE OF THE HEART

POETRY IS THE LANGUAGE OF THE HEART

POETRY IS THE LANGUAGE OF THE HEART

1. Poetry is the language of the heart, and philosophy is the language of the mind.
2. Plan as if you're living forever; live as if you're going to die today.
3. Do not do bad things that may haunt you forever, but do good things that will earn you respect and recognition.
4. Each person will be judged by how well he/she treats others.
5. Do your best where no one else can do any better.
6. Always finish your tasks; wasted time will never come back. Life gives you many options; do your best to make the right decision.
7. When the Lord is generous to you, be generous to others in the same way.
8. Respect gives you honor; kindness gives you humility.
9. Live within your own means and not within the means of others.

10. Treat other people with courtesy and respect even when they're gnashing their teeth at you.
11. Treat people with patience and caring; do not treat them with vengeance and hatred.
12. Friends are like inflated balloons; once you puncture them, they're gone!
13. Happiness is as elusive as the mirage of the desert; you think you have it, but you don't.
14. It vanishes before your eyes just like smoke.
15. Education, discipline, and a good attitude will take you to the top, but once you get there, remember how you got there.
16. Dreams will continue to be dreams unless you turn them into achievements.
17. When life turns against you, stay out of the way.
18. Do not ask others to do for you that you can do for yourself.
19. Procrastination is like stagnant water; it smells and does not go anywhere.
20. Do not accept mediocrity, for that will keep you at the bottom of the ladder.
21. The people who cause others pain and suffering shall suffer the same 100 times over.

PROVERBS ARE THE JOURNEY OF LIFE

STUDENTS WHO FALL ASLEEP

STUDENTS WHO FALL ASLEEP

JOHN A. SHALHOUB

STUDENTS WHO FALL ASLEEP

11 November 2002

1. Students who fall asleep in class will not pass.
2. Let your grades shoot up like rockets to the stars.
3. Don't let your grades crash like rockets falling to the ground.
4. Take advantage of your education—many children don't have the same opportunity.
5. Life is like a locked room; you don't know what's inside until you open the door.
6. Education is your best chance to make the most of your life.
7. The greatest calamity in life is failure.
8. Don't waste time trying to make sense of nonsense— think pragmatically.
9. Idleness leads to boredom; stay busy, and you won't be bored.
10. Whining is a sign of a hungry mind; replace whining with studying.
11. Whining, moaning, and complaining don't produce success—hard work does.

12. If you don't want to go anywhere, you won't get anywhere!
13. Stagnant water always smells.
14. Let your conscience be your compass and your mind your navigator.
15. Good judgment comes from common sense, and experience comes from bad decisions.
16. Overcoming difficulties to earn an A, B, or C is an accomplishment, but cheating for an A is not.
17. You have only one life—protect it from drugs, alcohol, and bad habits.
18. Respect is the ultimate honor of one's pride.
19. Those who harm others should expect the same in return. The truth always prevails, even if it takes a detour.
20. People who plot mischief will be trapped by their own schemes.
21. Being drug-free is the way to be!
22. Surrendering to evil perpetuates evil while standing by the truth perpetuates the truth.
23. Education is a ladder to higher responsibilities.
24. Corruption is the byproduct of greed.
25. Deception is the product of a corrupt mind.
26. False perception leads to a false reality.

27. To truly understand someone, speak heart to heart and mind to mind.
28. Money without compassion is an empty heart.
29. A true friend never turns their back on you.
30. Don't argue—seek answers to what you want to know.
31. Education is self-motivation.
32. Don't be the class clown because that's all you'll ever be.
33. Don't throw a stone into the well from which you just drank.
34. One student in the class is better than ten in prison!
35. Good guys may finish last, but they get further in life.
36. Information without focus is like a door without a key.

PROVERBS ARE THE JOURNEY OF LIFE

TRIGGERS TO IMPROVE LIFE!

TRIGGERS TO IMPROVE LIFE!

TRIGGERS TO IMPROVE LIFE

December 17, 2023

1. Psychological, spiritual, and inner development build your true personality and character.
2. Peace nurtures nations and people.
3. Hard work brings prosperity and sustenance.
4. Tranquility leads to serenity and inner comfort.
5. Kindness paves the way for meekness and friendship.
6. Blessings foster spiritual growth and divine grace.
7. A loving heart beats with a cheerful spirit.
8. Love fills you with joy, kindness, and a sweet personality.
9. Confidence fuels self-reliance.
10. Faith builds resilience and fosters a humble connection with God.
11. A happy personality helps you become friendlier with others.
12. Loyalty is the foundation of commitment and true friendship.

13. Faith is the source of patience in withstanding life's storms.
14. Divine grace energizes the soul and brings self-satisfaction.
15. Do not control others if you do not want to be controlled yourself.
16. Self-confidence inspires the courage to do honest work.
17. If you don't believe in God, you may not truly understand the hunger for spiritual nourishment.
18. Every day you look at the sky, you are reminded that you are alive on Earth.
19. Never doubt God's mercy; know that your heavenly reward will never be lost.
20. If you are faithful to God, He will know your thoughts and fulfill your needs—provided you are not lazy.
21. Do not challenge God's wisdom with human intelligence. No matter how long it takes, He remains true to those who are loyal to Him.
22. Even if your rights seem lost, God will restore them in His way and time.
23. Wisdom is the source of honesty, and honesty is the foundation of a genuine life.

24. My God rules the universe, and His wisdom endures forever.
25. My God, send peace, harmony, and security to humanity so we may live without war, violence, and tyranny.

PROVERBS ARE THE JOURNEY OF LIFE

KEYS FOR DOORS OF LIFE

KEYS FOR DOORS OF LIFE

JOHN A. SHALHOUB

KEYS FOR DOORS OF LIFE

26 June 2014

1. Smile at the world, and the world will open doors for you.
2. Life's hardships have no color, and bread shows no loyalty.
3. Ugliness and laziness isolate; the more you have, the lonelier you become.
4. Look to the stars, gaze beyond the horizon, and set yourself free.
5. Don't give up, even if you're ready to jump ship.
6. A nation that discards its skilled and talented people is doomed to fail.
7. Parents: always know where your children are and be their friends.
8. Students: always know where your books are and be loyal to them.
9. Teachers: understand your students and their needs.
10. Politicians: know your constituents and be grateful for their support.
11. Examine the quality before you buy—not after.
12. If the heat is too high, turn down the thermostat.
13. Education frees; ignorance binds in chains.

14. Time is as precious as air and water—use it wisely, and you will succeed.
15. Education gives vision, while ignorance blinds.
16. Seek peace, and you will live in peace; seek war, and you will die in it.
17. Hard work conquers obstacles; laziness conquers nothing.
18. Deception, pride, and vanity destroy—honesty and truth bring peace of mind.
19. Be positive, and you'll feel good all over!
20. Children: be proud, grow strong, work hard, and blossom like flowers.
21. Education is your path to success; you are the future.
22. Young men and women don't squander life; education shapes your destiny.
23. Victory is sweet when you love what you do.
24. Peace will prevail when prejudice and violence end.
25. Education gives you two doors: success and defeat; the choice is yours.
26. Education nourishes the mind as food nourishes the body.
27. Respect others to respect yourself.

JOHN A. SHALHOUB

COMMON AND POPULAR SAYINGS

COMMON AND POPULAR SAYINGS

PROVERBS ARE THE JOURNEY OF LIFE

COMMON AND POPULAR SAYINGS

July 29, 2024

1. One carries his beard, and the other is tired of it.
2. And whoever takes by the sword will be taken by the sword.
3. Haste leads to regret and laziness prolongs sleep.
4. If you are not forgiving, the crocodile will wipe you out.
5. Only your own nails will scratch your skin.
6. And only those who love you will hear your voice when you are in pain.
7. If you do not serve others, you are a hypocrite.
8. If a loaf of bread is for everyone, then so is forgiveness.
9. Woe to those who think they are better than others.
10. Money and peace are food for everyone who extends their hands to serve humanity.
11. If opportunity knocks on your door, seize it.
12. In the dark, there are surprises and in preparation, there is hope.

13. Secrets are made at night, and during the day, fire will burn.
14. There are enemies among friends; beware of them.
15. And on dark nights, the full moon will be missed.
16. If you offer me water, do not put poison in it.
17. Allow goodness to grow in your heart.
18. Good behavior is an image of your soul from the inside.
19. Focus on your work without stress.
20. Don't be, and don't imitate yourself with anyone else.
21. If you don't know what you want, continue your research until you get the answer.
22. Great things do not come easily.
23. Honor is like a crown on your head; it gives you pride.
24. Improve your attitude and change your behavior to be acceptable among your people.
25. Be humble and honest with yourself and others.
26. Don't harass people's lives, be kind.
27. If we do not learn from history, the same mistake will be repeated.

PROVERBS ARE THE JOURNEY OF LIFE

28. Do not interfere in the affairs of others.
29. New things are always enthusiastic and exciting.
30. Learn from wisdom and experience.
31. Practice improves your performance to achieve good results.
32. Hear and think and then speak.
33. Remember your manners and be kind to people.
34. Stay in school and do not be homeless on the streets.
35. Take advantage of opportunities and eventually, you will succeed.
36. Understand what you want to say and do.
37. Volunteer your time to do good deeds.
38. Work hard to help others.
39. Establish yourself in school and work.
40. Perseverance and not giving up are the best paths to success.
41. Your mind is your best friend; do not underestimate that.
42. Zero is zero; percent is percent; choose the best.

JOHN A. SHALHOUB

OH, MY SON

OH, MY SON

PROVERBS ARE THE JOURNEY OF LIFE

OH MY SON

28 December 2023

1. Consult your father and learn from his wisdom, drawn from countless sleepless nights and hard days. Through life's lessons, he has achieved much in culture, education, and work—striving without prejudice to provide you with shelter, food, and security.
2. Be a pillar for your father, as he has always been one for you, steadfast in both trials and triumphs.
3. Your father is your foundation; support him as he supports you. He is the cornerstone of the family, steadying you when life feels uncertain.
4. Learn from your father's knowledge and heed his advice, even when you believe you know better.
5. Respect your father as the head of the family. Be humble, kind, and polite, even if you feel more educated or knowledgeable.
6. It is your father who rises early and sleeps late to ensure you have comfort and

sustenance. He bears burdens so that yours may be lighter.
7. Your father takes pride in you, lifting you up so you may stand tall. Honor him as he honors you.
8. Never undermine or devalue your father, for he stands with you when life's storms come.
9. He is your rock, lifting you and looking to heaven, asking for blessings upon you.
10. He clears the road for you, securing the path so that you may reach your destination safely.
11. Be honest and truthful, my son. Do not mock or scorn anyone.
12. Remember, it is your father who raises his head each day and asks, "Son, how was your day?"
13. Walk the path he has prepared for you. Avoid the thorns and stones; follow the clear and steady roadways he has set.

PROVERBS ARE THE JOURNEY OF LIFE

CONTINUE ON YOUR WAY, DO NOT LOOK BACK!

CONTINUE ON YOUR WAY, DO NOT LOOK BACK!

JOHN A. SHALHOUB

CONTINUE ON YOUR WAY, DO NOT LOOK BACK!

6 March 1994

1. When hope leaves you, despair will visit you, and life appears to be worthless; a new spirit sprouts in your soul and inspires you to begin your journey.
2. When the road is full of pitfalls, the light turns into darkness, and the dangers multiply, a voice from within calls on you not to cancel your journey.
3. When anguish is intense, anxiety overwhelming and the heart is weary, a new energy surges in your heart to keep up with your journey.
4. When life is full of misery, the conscience of guilt and the mind of confusion, a light appears at the end of the tunnel to guide your journey.
5. When letdowns crush your spirit, frustrations your heart and failures your pride, this is the time you should continue
6. your journey.

7. When you are at the end of your rope, hanging by a thread and it is so dark around you, this is the time when the Lord will lift you up to wipe your tears and save you from falling.

JOHN A. SHALHOUB

PLAN YOUR LIFE TO LIVE A GOOD LIFE!

PLAN YOUR LIFE TO LIVE A GOOD LIFE!

PLAN YOUR LIFE TO LIVE A GOOD LIFE!

3 September 2022

Good learning is the road to success, honor, and integrity!

1. Plan your life, and you will get ahead in this world.
2. Your future is in your hands—do not surrender to laziness or failure.

3. Good teaching fosters creativity, innovation, and determination to make a difference in your life.

4. To achieve success as a learner, you must be willing to study, listen, and stay attentive.

5. Be inquisitive, motivated, and fully engaged in seeking answers to the questions that shape your future.

6. Education is the key to success and happiness in life.

7. Think deeply, focus, and be diligent in all you do, always acting with compassion and loving care.

JOHN A. SHALHOUB

POSITIVE SELF-TALK GIVES YOU STRENGTH

POSITIVE SELF-TALK GIVES YOU STRENGTH

POSITIVE SELF-TALK GIVES YOU STRENGTH!

11 October 2011

1. I am a valuable and unique individual, deserving of respect from others.

2. I approach life with optimism and eagerly embrace new challenges.

3. I am learning to be kind, truthful, patient, and compassionate.

4. I am growing more optimistic about achieving my goals.

5. I view temporary setbacks as stepping stones that build my character and strengthen my resolve.

6. I enjoy receiving compliments and love helping others gain recognition and credit for their efforts.

7. I feel warm, loving, and positive about myself.

8. I am unaffected by the negative opinions of others.

9. I take pride in giving my best, growing in awareness, and striving to meet my own high standards.

10. I measure my success by how loving I feel toward myself.

11. No one in the world is more important than I am.

12. No one in the world is less important than I am.

13. Every day, I make time to count my blessings.

14. I am learning to be productive and efficient.

15. I break large tasks into manageable steps, focusing on one thing at a time.

16. I am learning to be gentle, forgiving, and kind to myself.

17. I am learning not to worry.
18. If a problem can be addressed here and now, I will handle it; otherwise, I let it go.

19. I am learning to appreciate every moment of my life, avoiding dwelling on the past or an imagined future.

20. I am learning to love each moment of my life unconditionally.

21. I am beginning to understand that everyone and everything around me is a teacher.

22. I realize that being upset over what I lack wastes the appreciation of what I already have.

JOHN A. SHALHOUB

POOR MINDS, POOR POCKETS

POOR MINDS, POOR POCKETS

POOR MINDS, POOR POCKETS!

June 1, 2024

1. Poor money, poor life, poor education, lives in poverty.
2. Poor culture, poor background, can't get along with different people!
3. Poor skills, miserable life, hopeless outcome.
4. Each cooker has its own lid, and each cooker has its own size.
5. When salt spoils, the earth will be corrupted, and the corrupt people will be in control.
6. Even if one rises from the dead, they will mock him and jeer him as a hypocrite.
7. And when justice is asleep, unjust rulers will multiply, and justice will take a leave of absence.
8. When the oppressed people are dying, the tyrant oppressors will mock them.
9. When the sky weeps, the earth will overflow with tears.
10. Woe to the land over which the oppressors are in control and rule the land.

11. And when the land is drained of water, what will the peasants use to irrigate and cultivate their land?
12. And when injustice triumphs, darkness will cover the earth and humanity will live in darkness.
13. If the tyrants rule the workers, the land will dry out of its production and crops.
14. The people who dance now with joy will weep later during the reckoning day.
15. Every day has a night, every crime has a punishment, and every deception will be revealed.
16. And for every hill, there is a slope.
17. Every conflict has a resolution, and every problem has an answer.
18. And if you show off over other people, your value will be rejected and reduced wherever you walk.

PROVERBS ARE THE JOURNEY OF LIFE

IDEAL PROVERBS ARE RESOURCE FOR HONORABLE LIFE

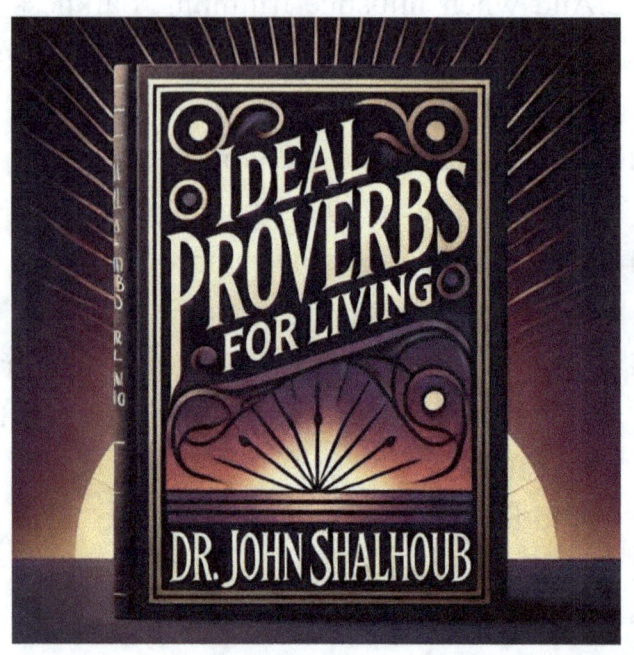

IDEAL PROVERBS ARE RESOURCE FOR HONORABLE LIFE

JOHN A. SHALHOUB

IDEAL PROVERBS ARE RESOURCE FOR HONORABLE LIFE

September 18, 2008

1.   The fool seeks water from the well without a bucket.

2.   He who ignores his people will die alone.

3.   He who walks on the bodies of the dead will be as dead as the rest.

4.   To ignore the one who fed and sheltered you is the mark of a traitor.

5.   Every arrogant soul meets their time, sooner or later.

6.   Even the greatest have someone greater than themselves.

7.   God's mercy cannot be received with pride.

8.   He who bites the dust will be buried in it.

9.   The victor is often the one who never enters the fight.

10. In conflict, absorb blows like a sponge or bend like a reed without breaking.

11. Humanity has achieved technological mastery, yet it lags in moral responsibility.

12. A student without knowledge is like a wheel without oil.

13. Age doesn't erase responsibility for one's actions.

14. Age matters less than the responsibility you take for your destiny.

15. He who ignores loyalty knows nothing of self-respect.

16. Those dissatisfied without pay will no longer be satisfied with it.

17. He who steals an egg would steal a camel.

18. The one who doesn't quit the race is the one who wins in the end.

19. The depth of one's soul is the path to communion with God.

JOHN A. SHALHOUB

TO THOSE WHO HAVE EARS AND EYE!

TO THOSE WHO HAVE EARS AND EYE!

PROVERBS ARE THE JOURNEY OF LIFE

TO THOSE WHO HAVE EARS AND EYE!

23 October 2021

1. Do not confide in a jealous person who cannot be trusted.

2. Do not turn your back on someone who might be ready to turn against you.

3. Avoid asking advice from someone ignorant in the area you seek unless they show a desire for knowledge and growth.

4. Seek guidance from those with more knowledge and experience; learn from their wisdom.

5. Always be honest and truthful in your dealings with others.

6. Do not argue with stubborn people unless they show flexibility and understanding.

7. Seek knowledge from those who are tolerant, flexible, and patient.

8. Avoid arrogance and showing off; instead, be humble, kind, and friendly.

9. Humility is the foundation of friendship, and friendship is the source of honesty and truth.

10. Do not challenge those who may be stronger than you.

11. Avoid befriending hypocrites; always be truthful and straightforward in your dealings.

12. Do not entrust your secrets to those who cannot even keep their own.

13. A person's value is not defined by religious affiliation but by tolerance, acceptance, and a commitment to peace.

14. Those who seek harm for others will ultimately harvest suffering.

15. God embodies love and peace, not revenge; He offers love and forgiveness.

16. God gives us countless opportunities to repent and seek forgiveness—it's up to us to open the door for Him.

17. Dear Lord, guide us away from evil.

18. Protect us from illness and disease and open the door to everlasting life.

19. Shield us from harm and help us recognize that You are a loving God of peace, forgiveness, and enlightenment.

Amen.

JOHN A. SHALHOUB

PROVERBS & PERCEPTION OF LIFE

PROVERBS & PERCEPTION OF LIFE

PROVERBS & PERCEPTION OF LIFE

14 October 1971

1. A house without a wife is like a lake without water
2. No man ever dies, and another does not fill
3. his place.
4. No man was ever born and does not add up to the falling tears of the world
5. '''No man ever is planning and does not lose his temper under severe stress.
6. No nation is ever successful without imposing burdens upon its own citizens.
7. The faith of a good man is honesty and truth.
8. Many people marry to avoid loneliness, and many others may marry because it is the destination of life.
9. People fear life because they are unable to foresee the future.
10. No person is fully in control of his life, even because
11. he cannot read the future.
12. Happiness is an idealistic concept. It exists only on paper or in the mind.
13. The woman who lacks faith in her husband lacks faith in herself.
14. The man who neglects his wife neglects himself.

15. Beauty of the skin is like a withering flower.
16. A human being can be full of pride, ignorance, and selfishness, but humility can transform him into a wonderful personality.
17. God is for man and man is for God and both need each other to fulfill the mission of life.
18. No person ever cries and does not leave a scar on someone's heart!
19. No person ever returns to this earth after he leaves it.
20. The infinite wisdom of life may carry him into another infinite place in the infinite universe.

PROVERBS ARE THE JOURNEY OF LIFE

DAILY WORDS INSPIRATION FOR LIVING

DAILY WORDS INSPIRATION FOR LIVING

JOHN A. SHALHOUB

DAILY WORDS OF INSPIRATION FOR LIVING

12 August 2024

1.   Never doubt your ability to perform well! You are the fruits of life; be the seeds of the future!

2.   Character is your road to honor and integrity!

3.   Plan and you will get ahead. The future is in your hands!

4.   Good teaching is the ability to be creative, innovative, and determined to make a difference in a person's life.

5.   Character is the fiber that glues your life to be happy, fulfilled, and content.

6.   Education is the willingness to gain knowledge and apply it in a constructive way.

7.   Hope, ambition, courage, respect, caring, and sharing.

8.   Good character is the map for a better life! Character is the foundation of success!

9.   Character is the key to success: Honesty, integrity, responsibility, fairness, loyalty, citizenship, and trustworthiness.

10.   These traits and thoughts will enrich your mind and heart so that you can do well every day and succeed in your job, at home, and at work.

JOHN A. SHALHOUB

WORDS OF WISDOM ARE WISDOM

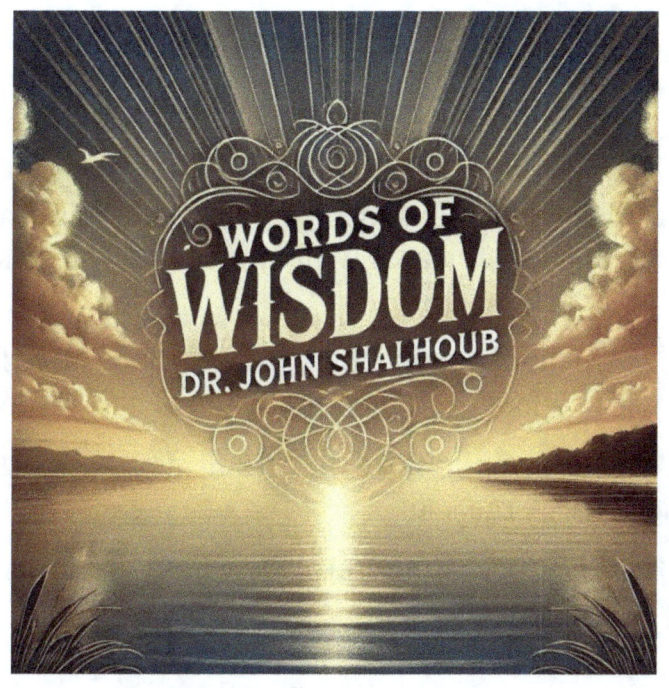

WORDS OF WISDOM ARE WISDOM

WORDS OF WISDOM ARE WISDOM

18 January 2022

1. He who speaks wisdom is the one who enjoys the benefits of grace.

2. He who enjoys the benefits of blessing is the one whom God pleases with him because he shares his grace with others.

3. But those who boast of arrogance will fall into arrogance with ignorance.

4. The simplicity of the heart stems from the innocence of the soul.

5. He who speaks the truth will enjoy the fruits of the truth.

6. He who lives in anger will suffer 7. from anger.

8. Tolerance is the outcome of self-fulfillment and contentment.

9. Be honest, fair, and optimistic.

10. Ask for happiness for those who seek fairness, justice, and compassion.

11. Each of us has a place in this world, and each of us has a position in society.

12. Each of us has goals that should be accomplished.

13. We all must fulfill what God has appointed for our lives.

CHAPTER FIVE
EDUCATION IS THE KEY FOR SUCCESS

Learning is gaining knowledge and applying it in a constructive way!

JOHN A. SHALHOUB

THEMES OF BEHAVIOR FOR EVERY DAY

THEMES OF BEHAVIOR FOR EVERY DAY

THEMES OF BEHAVIOR FOR EVERY DAY

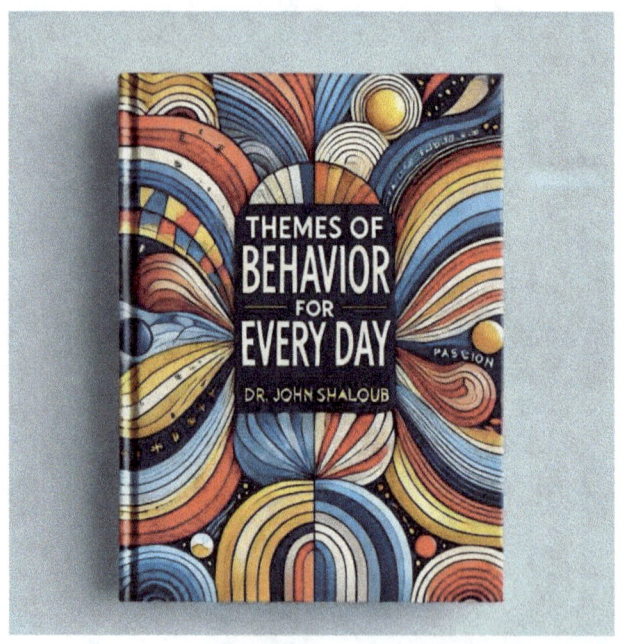

15 August 996

DAILY THEMES:

Honesty shines like gold!

Together, we build a stable and happy world!

Integrity embodies honor and grace!

Loyalty brings inner peace!

Monday: Integrity and Cooperation

- Honor and decency are the foundations of true integrity.
- Collaborate with others; share your talents freely.
- Education and honesty lead to true freedom.
- Respect the rules, uphold the law, and honor those in authority. ·

Tuesday: Trust and Teamwork · Trust in God, yourself, and the truth.

- Teamwork makes progress possible.
- Present your best self in everything you do.
- Help others and experience the joy of giving.
·

Wednesday: Perseverance and Gratitude

- Stay committed and don't look back.
- Keep pushing forward; success awaits those who don't quit.
- Return borrowed items and show gratitude.

- Keep your space tidy and don't leave a mess behind.
-

Thursday: Honesty and Responsibility

- Be truthful; avoid lies and dishonesty.
- Respect the opinions of others and practice empathy.
- Be a loyal friend.
- Avoid unnecessary conflicts.
- Contribute your fair share; don't pass your duties onto others.
-

Friday: Truthfulness and Accountability · Always tell the truth; honesty leads to victory.

- Strive for excellence and achieve your goals.
- Keep your promises and honor your commitments.
- Care for the environment and practice recycling.
-

Saturday: Perseverance and Community · Persist and persevere; don't waver from your path.

- Be open to advice and manage your time wisely.
- Offer a helping hand to friends.
- Be a considerate neighbor.

- Protect the earth; it belongs to all of us.
-

Sunday: Reflection and Spirituality

- Trust yourself and continue working hard.
- Reflect on your actions and learn from them.
- Practice spirituality with grace and compassion.
- God's grace embodies love and kindness.
- Remember, God is universal; live in a way that honors Him.

PROVERBS ARE THE JOURNEY OF LIFE

HONESTY AND TRUTH ARE THE FOUNDATION FOR GOOD PEOPLE!

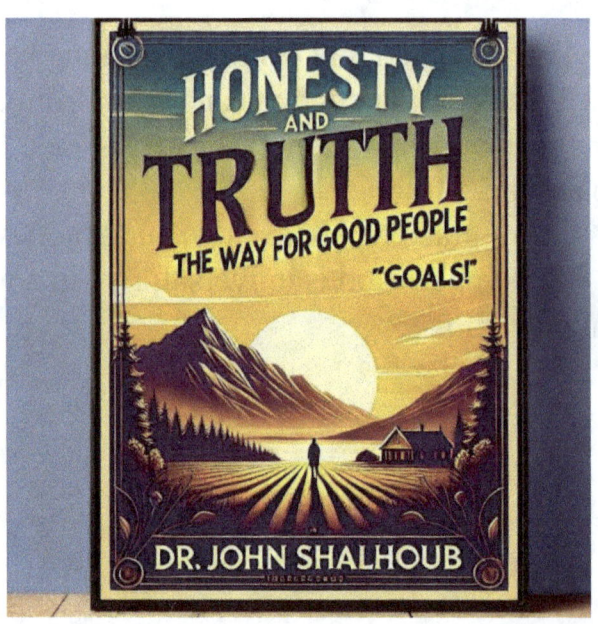

HONESTY AND TRUTH ARE THE FOUNDATION FOR GOOD PEOPLE!

JOHN A. SHALHOUB

HONESTY AND TRUTH ARE FOUNDATION FOR GOOD PEOPLE!

3 March 2005

DAILY THEMES: Honesty shines like gold!

Together, we build a stable and happy world.

Integrity embodies honor and grace. Loyalty grants inner peace.

Monday: Honor and decency are the pillars of integrity.

- Work with others; share your skills generously.
- Truth and education go hand in hand—they set you free.
- Respect rules, uphold the law, and value authority.

Tuesday: Trust in God, the truth, and yourself.

- Teamwork achieves great things.
- Strive to look your best, do your best, and be your best.

- Offer help to others; the joy of giving is its own reward.

Wednesday: Stay committed and don't look back.
- Persevere, and victory will be yours.
- Return borrowed items with gratitude.
- Keep your space tidy; don't leave a mess behind.

Thursday: Be honest—don't lie or cheat.
- Respect other people's opinions.
- Be a true friend.
- Avoid unnecessary arguments.
- Do your share of work; don't pass the responsibility to others.

Friday: Speak the truth and reap the rewards.
- Always give your best effort to achieve your goals.
- Honor your commitments and promises.
- Care for the environment—practice recycling.

Saturday: Persist and persevere; stay the course.

- Be open to advice and make the most of your time.
- Offer a helping hand to friends.
- Be a considerate neighbor.
- Protect the earth—it belongs to us all.

Sunday: Trust yourself and continue putting in the hard work.

- Reflect on your actions and learn from them.
- Embrace spirituality and embody grace.
- Remember, God's love is compassion itself.
- Honor God by being good; don't let Him down.

PROVERBS ARE THE JOURNEY OF LIFE

LOYALTY, KINDNESS, RESPECT, HONOR!

LOYALTY, KINDNESS, RESPECT, HONOR!

JOHN A. SHALHOUB

PERSEVERANCE PRODUCES PATIENCE

PERSEVERANCE PRODUCES PATIENCE

PROVERBS ARE THE JOURNEY OF LIFE

PERSEVERANCE PRODUCE PATIENCE

25 February 2002

Daily Themes

- Be kind and polite, and others will respond in kind.
- Speak the truth to find inner peace.
- Respect others' feelings and viewpoints.
- Be ready to help those in need.
- A sense of security and peace will follow.

Monday

- Persevere and stay skillful, especially in difficult situations.
- Always keep your promises.
- Offer kindness without expecting anything in return.
- Remember, honesty is its own reward.

Tuesday

- Help others break free from oppression.

- Be honest so that people can rely on you.
- Build trust by being responsible and dependable.

Wednesday

- Show compassion; if someone is hurt, check on them.
- Stay focused when given a task.
- Believe in yourself and strive to achieve your dreams.

Thursday

- Offer help in any way you can, day by day.
- Show care and support to those who need it.
- Be truthful in all that you do.

Friday

- Lead by example instead of following the crowd.
- Respect the rules.
- Keep a positive attitude and work well with others.

- Be honest.

Saturday

- Reliability and truthfulness can change your life.
- Complete your tasks and be helpful at home.
- Avoid making fun of others or being unkind.

Sunday

- Spend time doing what brings you joy.
- Treat others with the same respect you'd want for yourself.
- Be kind, humble, and truthful.
- Remember, honesty sets you free, and with faith, you'll find strength.

JOHN A. SHALHOUB

CHARACTER EDUCATION IS LIKE THE RUNNING WATER OF FERTILE LAND

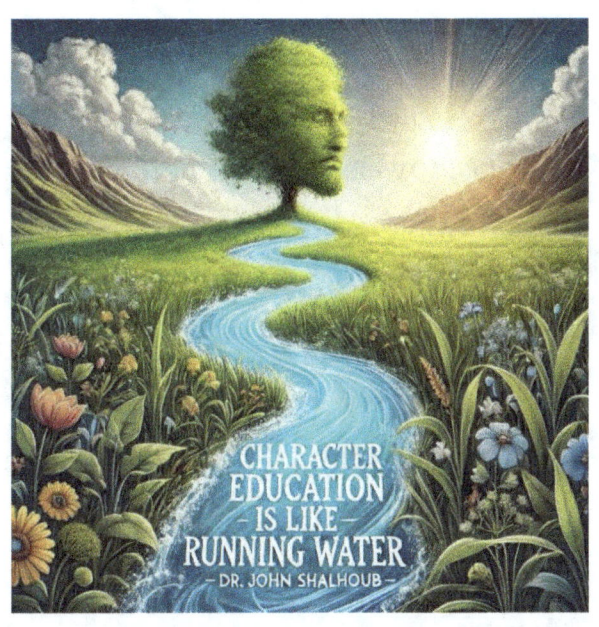

CHARACTER EDUCATION IS LIKE THE RUNNING WATER OF FERTILE LAND

PROVERBS ARE THE JOURNEY OF LIFE

CHARACTER EDUCATION IS LIKE RUNNING WATER OF FERTILE LAND

8 June 2008

Daily Themes

- Fairness: Strive to be truthful and show tolerance towards others' needs.
- Organization: Keep your life ordered and purposeful.
- Compassion: Show mercy to family and friends; treat them with kindness.
- Loyalty: Be faithful to those close to you, and they will support you in return.

Monday

- Show kindness to family and friends.
- Think before you act, and set personal goals.
- Share your skills with those eager to learn.
- Be dependable, reliable, and accountable.

Tuesday

- Accept people as they are, regardless of wealth or status.
- Walk away from violence.
- Do not repay evil with evil.
- Strive to do good consistently, fairly, and with effort.

Wednesday

- Avoid judging others.
- Take responsibility and complete your work.
- Treat others with dignity and respect.

Thursday

- Look for the good in everyone.
- Take pride in your achievements.
- Be helpful to family and friends.
- Stay focused and don't let laziness interfere with your goals.

Friday

- Be honest with others.

- Choose kind words in all interactions.
- Learn from your mistakes.
- If you can't say something positive, hold back.
- Doing what's right will bring happiness.

Saturday

- Stay committed to your goals and values.
- Do your best in all things.
- Take initiative and act with integrity.
- Treat others as you want to be treated.
- Stand by the truth, and it will support you in return.

Sunday

- Good work brings rewards wherever it is done.
- Be a responsible citizen and encourage others to do what's right.
- Follow sound advice to find success.

- Remember that true victory lies in avoiding harmful habits like drugs, alcohol, and gambling.

PROVERBS ARE THE JOURNEY OF LIFE

LIVE WELL EVERY DAY!

LIVE WELL EVERY DAY!

LIVE WELL EVERY DAY

21 January 2009

Daily Themes

Feel important, live with integrity, tell the truth, do your best, and be helpful! Organize your life thoughtfully and strive for a meaningful, balanced week.

Monday: Personal Growth and Compassion

- Value yourself and set goals to reach your full potential.
- Share with others; generosity is fulfilling.

Tuesday: Patience and Positivity

- Practice patience and wisdom in your actions.
- Think before reacting; avoid impulsive choices.
- Stay positive and truthful to earn respect from others.

- Listen to your conscience and let it guide your heart.
- Show empathy and be considerate of others' experiences.

Wednesday: Respect and Responsibility

- Treat everyone with fairness and honesty.
- Be kind, supportive, and trustworthy.
- Complete tasks on time—don't procrastinate!
- Remember that actions have consequences; be mindful of how you treat others.

Thursday: Self-Control and Citizenship

- Manage your temper and choose kindness over anger.
- Be a respectful, law-abiding citizen.
- Honesty builds trust; people appreciate sincerity.

- Show gratitude to those who lend a helping hand.
- Support your parents when they need you.

Friday: Kindness and Self-Respect

- Use kind words and avoid hurting others.
- Share what you have to make others feel valued.
- Keep a healthy routine: rest well and rise early.
- Show respect for the law and support your community.

Saturday: Politeness and Planning

- Always be courteous and polite to everyone.
- Avoid harmful substances; they can derail your dreams.
- Honor and listen to your parents.
- Plan your day to stay organized and succeed.

PROVERBS ARE THE JOURNEY OF LIFE

CHARACTER IS THE SALT OF GOOD BEHAVIOR

CHARACTER IS THE SALT OF GOOD BEHAVIOR

JOHN A. SHALHOUB

CHARACTER IS THE SALT OF GOOD BEHAVIOR

25 February 2002

Daily Themes

Organizing your life with intention and purpose sets the foundation for growth and success.

Monday: Perseverance and Integrity

- Stay determined and resourceful, especially in difficult times.
- Keep your promises, no matter how small.
- When helping others, expect nothing in return.
- Remember, honesty is always worth it.

Tuesday: Honesty and Dependability

- Support others who are facing hardship or oppression.
- Be honest and reliable so people know they can count on you.

- Show trustworthiness by taking on responsibilities with integrity.

Wednesday: Compassion and Commitment

- Show care for others—if someone is hurt, offer comfort.
- Focus when given a task and complete it responsibly.
- Believe in yourself and work toward your dreams with confidence.

Thursday: Helping and Caring

- Make helping others a regular habit.
- Show compassion and extend help to those who need it.
- Keep honesty at the core of your actions.

Friday: Leadership and Positivity

- Lead by example and choose the right path over simply following.

- Respect the rules and encourage others to do the same.
- Maintain a positive attitude and work well with others.
- Honesty is a quality that builds trust.

Saturday: Reliability and Respect

- Being truthful and dependable positively shapes your life.
- Complete your tasks and contribute at home.
- Avoid mocking or being unkind to others.

Sunday: Joy and Integrity

- Spend time on activities that bring you happiness.
- Treat others with the respect you'd want for yourself.
- Be kind, humble, and honest in all you do.
- The truth brings freedom, and strength comes from living with integrity.

INTEGRITY AND PEACE FOR TOMORROW

INTEGRITY AND PEACE FOR TOMORROW

JOHN A. SHALHOUB

INTEGRITY AND PEACE FOR TOMORROW

By

Dr. Fr. John Shalhoub

15 September 2003

Daily Themes

- **Core Values:** Caring, respect, integrity, fellowship, and safety.
- Listen attentively and be present in every moment.
- Keep your surroundings clean; avoid littering.

Monday: Caring and Respect

- Show care for your family and friends, and they'll care for you.
- Respect others, and they will respect you in return.
- Handle all property with care—never damage what belongs to someone else.

Tuesday: Kindness and Honesty

- Be kind and respectful to help friendships grow.
- Speak positively about others; kindness attracts kindness.
- Be truthful with yourself and harbor no ill will toward anyone.
- Avoid actions that hurt or annoy others.
- Treat people with gentleness and enjoy the good feeling it brings.

Wednesday: Compassion and Gratitude

- Show compassion and offer help when it's needed.
- Appreciate your blessings and value what you have.
- Give your best effort in everything you do.
- Remember: Knowledge brings opportunity—keep learning and growing!
- Excel in school and earn the pride of your family.

Thursday: Honor and Peace

- Be a considerate and helpful neighbor.
- Treat people with kindness and respect.
- Strive to be honorable and trustworthy.
- Value truth, and it will guide you.
- Avoid trouble, and trouble will avoid you.

Friday: Integrity and Forgiveness

- Avoid gossip and stay truthful.
- Speaking disrespectfully can lead to resentment; be mindful.
- Show respect and kindness to everyone.
- Be friendly, and happiness will follow you through the day.
- Practice forgiveness—it brings peace of mind.
- Release grudges to keep your conscience clear.

Saturday: Friendship and Responsibility

- Be a good friend, and friendship will find you.
- Don't flirt with trouble or negativity.
- Stay away from fights and arguments.
- Be a peacemaker, spreading harmony.

Sunday: Politeness and Obedience

- Resolve disagreements calmly, without arguments.
- Show love and respect to your parents, and they'll treat you kindly.
- Listen to teachers without interruption.
- Avoid being rude or disruptive; aim for politeness.
- Use a calm voice—everyone can hear you without yelling.

JOHN A. SHALHOUB

CHARACTER EDUCATION GIVES YOU DIGNITY

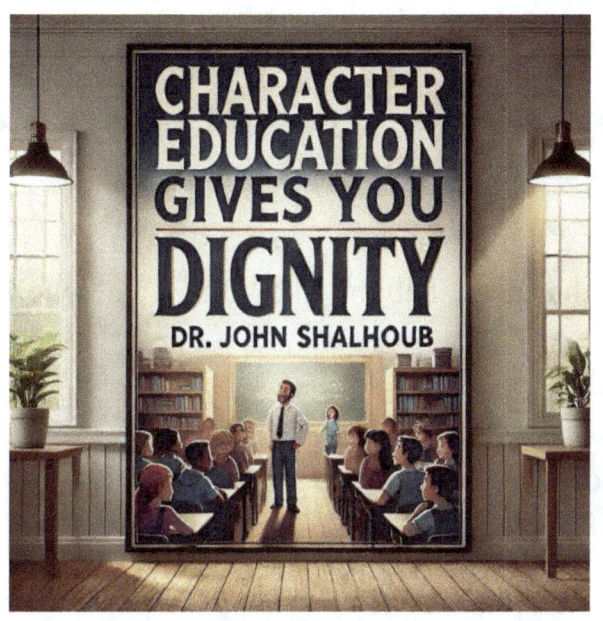

CHARACTER EDUCATION GIVES YOU DIGNITY

CHARACTER EDUCATION GIVES YOU DIGNITY

15 September 2005

Daily Themes: Fairness, Organization, Compassion, Faithfulness

- Winning in life means staying away from harmful habits like drugs, alcohol, and gambling.

Monday: Kindness and Accountability

- Be kind to family and friends—they're your foundation.
- Think carefully before acting; set thoughtful goals for yourself.
- Share your knowledge with others who are eager to learn.
- Be dependable, reliable, and accountable in all your actions.

Tuesday: Acceptance and Peace

- Accept others for who they are, regardless of wealth or status.
- Walk away from violence and avoid seeking revenge.
- Strive to do good consistently, treating everyone equally.
- Take pride in doing a good job and being fair.

Wednesday: Responsibility and Respect

- Refrain from judging others; focus on improving your own actions.
- Be responsible—complete your work with dedication and care.
- Treat everyone with dignity and respect.

Thursday: Positivity and Diligence

- Look for the good in everyone you meet.
- Take pride in achieving your personal goals.
- Be helpful to family and friends; stay committed to your responsibilities.

- Avoid procrastination—stay focused and finish your tasks.

Friday: Honesty and Reflection

- Speak kindly and be honest with others.
- Learn from your mistakes—they are valuable lessons.
- If you cannot say something positive, it's better to remain silent.
- Do what is right, and happiness will follow.

Saturday: Faithfulness and Integrity

- Stay true to your goals and ideals.
- Take initiative and always act with integrity.
- Treat others as you would like to be treated.
- Stand up for the truth, and it will stand by you.

Sunday: Good Citizenship and Wisdom

- Hard work bears fruit wherever it is planted.
- Be a responsible citizen; inspire others to do what is right.
- Follow wise advice to guide your path to success.

PROVERBS ARE THE JOURNEY OF LIFE

CHARACTER COUNTS EVERYDAY

CHARACTER COUNTS EVERYDAY

JOHN A. SHALHOUB

CHARACTER COUNTS EVERYDAY

15 April 2004

Themes: Courage, Integrity, Cooperation, Trust, Citizenship

- Practice kindness and respect to be a good neighbor.
- Work towards making the world a happier and better place.

Monday: Integrity and Honesty

- Stand up for the truth and take pride in who you are.
- Always be truthful—avoid telling lies.
- Strive to maintain harmony and peace within your family.
- Be honest and loyal in all your actions.

Tuesday: Faithfulness and Accountability

- Train your mind to choose the right path, even when it's difficult.

- Show loyalty and respect to your family and friends.
- Stay calm and composed if things don't go your way.
- Keep your promises—they build the foundation of trust.
- Learn from your mistakes and use them as a stepping stone for growth.

Wednesday: Courage and Fairness

- Seek knowledge with confidence—don't fear setbacks.
- Stay honest; never steal or cheat.
- Be part of the solution, not the problem.
- Stand up for what is right, even when it's hard.
- Respect the rights of others and treat everyone fairly.

Thursday: Determination and Teamwork

- Persevere, even when faced with challenges.
- Show respect to elders, parents, and those guiding you.
- Embrace teamwork—it leads to success and growth.
- Work diligently, even when no one is watching.
- Respect the law—it will protect you in return.

Friday: Responsibility and Perseverance

- Strive to become the best version of yourself.
- Listen to coaches, mentors, and leaders with respect.
- Finish what you start, and if you fail, try again.
- Focus on your goals with heart and integrity.
- Honor your country and contribute to its well-being.

Saturday: Discipline and Honor

- Use discipline and organization to achieve new heights.
- Spend your leisure time on positive and meaningful activities.
- Begin each day with the goal of doing good work.
- Integrity and honesty are the foundation of a life of honor.
- Protect and value your country, and it will protect you in return.

Sunday: Reflection and Renewal

- Reflect on your actions and find ways to improve.
- Review your progress and set new goals for growth.
- Cherish time with family and create joyful moments together.

- Strive to do good every day and learn to forgive.
- Take responsibility for your actions.
- Place your trust in God, Jesus, and yourself.

PROVERBS ARE THE JOURNEY OF LIFE

CHARACTER SHINES LIKE A STAR OVERHEAD

CHARACTER SHINES LIKE A STAR OVERHEAD

10 NOVEMBER 2008

Daily Themes:

- Do your best, and you will become one of the best!
- Enrich your deeds with good values.
- Look forward to better things in life.
- Complete your tasks on time; avoid procrastination!

Monday: Don't Let Laziness Hold You Back—Complete Your Work on Time

- Stay focused and complete your tasks without delay.
- Laziness can hold you back—choose to be productive instead.
- Take pride in finishing what you start.

Tuesday: Set Meaningful Goals for Yourself and Work to Achieve Them

- Define clear, achievable goals and take consistent action.

- Each day brings an opportunity to move closer to what you want.
- Stay determined and keep striving.

Wednesday: Monitor Your Progress Regularly

- Regularly review your work and keep track of your goals.
- Learn from any setbacks and use them to improve.
- Be fair and generous with others; share your time and talents.

Thursday: Pursue Education Now and Appreciate It Later

- Be prepared and ready to learn.
- Education opens doors and leads to opportunities.
- Stay organized and responsible for your learning.

Friday: Finish Your Tasks and Stay Committed

- Follow through on your commitments and see your tasks through to completion.
- Ask for help if needed, and stay focused on your goals.
- Keep working hard and stay dedicated.

Saturday: Always See Your Work Through to the End

- Don't waste time; make every moment count.
- Complete tasks with care and attention.
- Aim to grow through hard work and responsibility.

Sunday: Remember, You Are Special, and So Are Your Friends

- Cherish your friends and treat others with kindness.
- Face challenges with courage, learning as you go.

- Discipline helps you stay organized and focused.
- Fill your mind with wisdom and knowledge—always keep learning.

JOHN A. SHALHOUB

RESPECT IS THE HEART OF GOOD BEHAVIOR

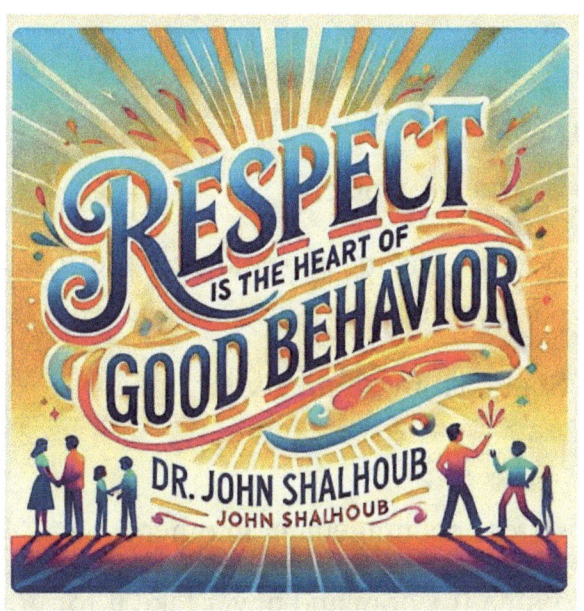

RESPECT IS THE HEART OF GOOD BEHAVIOR

PROVERBS ARE THE JOURNEY OF LIFE

RESPECT IS THE HEART OF GOOD BEHAVIOR

05 September 2005

DAILY THEMES:

- Be true to yourself.
- Avoid laziness—embrace effort and perseverance.
- Stand out by shining your light.
- Never give up.
- Offer encouragement to others.
- Value freedom and never take it for granted.

Monday: Citizenship and Responsibility

- Show respect for the law and demonstrate patriotism.
- Be honest, even when faced with challenges.
- Stand on your own two feet—be independent.

- Stand up to bullies and treat others with kindness.
- Let your smile be a welcoming sign.

Tuesday: Loyalty and Determination

- Practice respect, responsibility, and honesty in all you do.
- Honesty builds a strong foundation for life.
- Be loyal to your family and show yourself to be trustworthy.
- Bring cheer and kindness into the world; avoid negativity.
- Never give up—keep pushing forward.
- Embrace who you are.

Wednesday: Politeness and Respect

- Mind your manners.
- Avoid interrupting others and don't talk back to your parents.

- Show obedience and respect for those guiding you.
- Treat others with kindness and fairness.
- Avoid nagging and listen to your teachers.
- Be fair honest, and avoid copying others' work.

Thursday: Respect and Fairness

- Be kind and avoid mean-spirited actions.
- Don't call others names.
- Respect yourself and those around you.
- Complete your work and avoid being disruptive.
- Don't bully or boast—treat everyone fairly.

Friday: Politeness and Integrity

- Use polite language like "please" and "thank you."
- Honor honesty and resist the urge to cheat.

- Be kind to your friends, avoiding hurtful words or actions.
- Show respect with "Yes, sir" and "Yes, ma'am."
- Avoid talking with your mouth full and obey your elders.
- Don't ridicule or tease others.

Saturday: Self-Respect and Pride

- Keep your hands to yourself and maintain cleanliness.
- Work for what you need; don't rely on begging.
- Apologize when necessary and use polite phrases like "excuse me."
- Take pride in everything you do.
- Wise people make wise decisions—seek wisdom.
- Always demand the best from yourself.

Sunday: Integrity and Wisdom

- Remember: lying is like rust—it can corrode you from within.

- Accept responsibility for your actions to gain respect.

- Dedication and inspiration bring you closer to success.

- Take your time; haste can lead to waste.

- Surround yourself with good people who uplift you.

JOHN A. SHALHOUB

WE STAND FOR GOOD EDUCATION AND SUCCESS!

WE STAND FOR GOOD EDUCATION AND SUCCESS!

PROVERBS ARE THE JOURNEY OF LIFE

WE STAND FOR GOOD EDUCATION AND SUCCESS

7 October 2010

DAILY THEMES:

- Character counts every day of the week.
- The truth will set you free!
- Kindness begets kindness.
- Respect rules, obey the law, and live in peace.
- Eat well, stay healthy, and keep clean.
- Good manners shape strong character.

Monday: Respect and Responsibility

- Be kind and respectful to everyone.
- Treat others with dignity.
- Raise your hand before speaking in class.
- Keep your space tidy and get a good night's sleep.
- Show politeness to family and friends.

Tuesday: Listening and Learning

- Listen to your parents—it eases life's challenges.
- Follow your parents' guidance.
- Brush your teeth before bed.
- Spend time reading every day.
- Show respect to everyone.

Wednesday: Focus and Fairness

- Obey your parents and follow their instructions.
- Avoid using hurtful words.
- Remember, school is for learning, not fooling around.
- Pay attention to your teachers.
- Be gentle with others—no pushing or shoving.

Thursday: Honesty and Hard Work

- Appreciate the food you're given.
- Speak honestly; don't tell lies.
- Keep your tone calm and respectful.
- Understand when parents can't buy everything.
- Always give your best effort—hard work brings success.

Friday: Standards and Self-Respect

- Don't argue with your mom—listen with respect.
- Set high standards and aim to meet them.
- Be ambitious, not lazy.
- Stay clean and dress neatly.
- Practice respectful listening.

Saturday: Responsibility and Family Time

- Complete your homework and hand it in on time.
- Plan your tasks to avoid boredom.
- Help with household chores.
- Make time to enjoy your family.

Sunday: Gratitude and Joy

- Life is beautiful—celebrate it!
- Be grateful and express thanks.
- Honor and respect your family.
- Always strive to be your best.

EDUCATION IS YOUR GUIDING POST
FOR A BETTER LIFE *

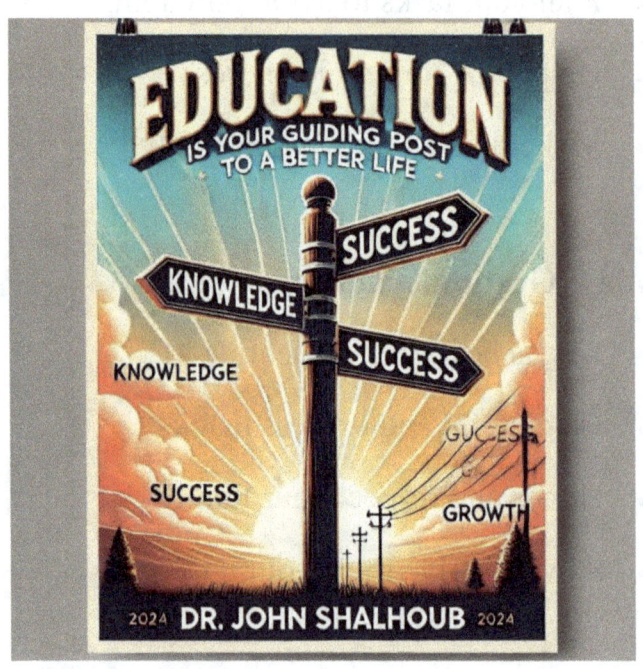

EDUCATION IS YOUR GUIDING POST
FOR A BETTER LIFE *

JOHN A. SHALHOUB

YOUR EDUCATION IS YOUR GUIDING POST FOR A BETTER LIFE

7 January 2004

DAILY THEMES: Be Important!

- Do the right thing, feel right, tell the truth!
- Do your best in everything you do.
- Be helpful whenever you can.

Monday: Believe in Yourself and Set Goals

- Practice generosity; learn to share.
- Always tell the truth to earn respect.
- Be considerate of others' feelings.
- Offer help to those in need.

Tuesday: Patience and Positivity

- Be patient; avoid acting impulsively.
- Keep a positive attitude to boost your happiness.
- Speak truthfully to gain respect.

- Listen to your conscience and be honest with yourself.
- Avoid harming others; let your conscience guide you.

Wednesday: Respect and Fairness

- Treat others with respect.
- Be fair and honest in all your interactions.
- Show kindness, be helpful, and support others.
- Stay trustworthy—avoid lying or cheating.
- Complete your work on time and don't procrastinate.
- Remember, if you mistreat others, they may do the same to you.

Thursday: Control and Responsibility

- Control your temper; avoid anger.
- Be a responsible citizen and respect the law.
- Stay honest, and people will trust you.
- Always thank those who help you.

- If your parents need assistance, give it willingly—don't give them a hard time.

Friday: Positivity and Effort

- Avoid using hurtful words; don't be mean.
- Share your skills with others and encourage them.
- Strive to do everything to the best of your ability.
- Be proud of your achievements.
- Keep a healthy routine by going to bed and waking up on time.
- Respect the law and support your community.

Saturday: Kindness and Respect

- Be kind and polite to everyone.
- Stay away from drugs; they are dangerous.
- Honor and listen to your parents.
- Organize your tasks and plan.
- Show respect to elders and supervisors.

Sunday: Responsibility and Manners

- Avoid talking back to your parents.
- Learn a skill—it can be your key to self-reliance.
- Don't take what isn't yours.
- Practice good manners; avoid rudeness.
- Stay away from drugs and never drink and drive.

JOHN A. SHALHOUB

CHARACTER BUILDS YOUR PERSONALITY UP!

EDUCATION IS YOUR GUIDING POST
FOR A BETTER LIFE *

CHARACTER BUILDS YOUR PERSONALITY UP!

15 August 2009

DAILY THEMES:

- **Organization** is arranging your life in an orderly way.
- **Compassion** is caring for family and friends and treating them kindly.
- **Loyalty** means being faithful and dependable to those you love.

MONDAY: Planning and Accountability

- Think before you act; plan for your future.
- Share your skills with those eager to learn.
- Be dependable, reliable, and accountable.

TUESDAY: Fairness and Effort

- Walk away from conflict.
- Don't repay negativity with negativity.

- Be fair and consistent in all you do.
- Always put in your best effort.

WEDNESDAY: Peace and Responsibility

- Let peace guide you and be a peacemaker.
- Treat everyone with dignity and respect.
- Be responsible for your actions.
- Perform your duties with faithfulness.

THURSDAY: Accomplishment and Focus

- Feel proud of your accomplishments.
- Be helpful to family and friends.
- Stay focused, complete your tasks, and avoid laziness.

FRIDAY: Reflection and Integrity

- Learn from life's challenges.
- If you have nothing good to say, say nothing.
- Do what is right, and happiness will follow.

SATURDAY: Initiative and Truth

- Take initiative; choose the right path.
- Treat others as you wish to be treated.
- Stand for truth, and truth will stand by you.

SUNDAY: Citizenship and Wisdom

- Be a good citizen; encourage others to do the right thing.
- Follow wise advice for a fulfilling life.
- True success means staying away from drugs, alcohol, and gambling.

JOHN A. SHALHOUB

CHAPTER SIX
A, B, C

EDUCATION IS YOUR ROAD TO HONOR AND INTEGRITY!

PROVERBS ARE THE JOURNEY OF LIFE

EDUCATION IS YOUR ROAD TO HONOR AND INTEGRITY!

PLAN AHEAD AND YOU WILL GET AHEAD.

THE FUTURE IS IN YOUR HANDS!

GOOD TEACHING IS THE ABILITY TO BE CREATIVE, INNOVATIVE, AND DETERMINED TO MAKE A DIFFERENCE IN A STUDENT'S LIFE.

JOHN A. SHALHOUB

INSTRUCT A FOOL AND HE WILL MOCK YOU!

INSTRUCT A FOOL AND HE WILL MOCK YOU!

PROVERBS ARE THE JOURNEY OF LIFE

INSTRUCT A FOOL AND HE WILL MOCK YOU!

15 JANUARY 2003

A. Advise a fool, and he may only mimic you.
B. Be all you can be, with honor and integrity.
C. Cooperate with others, and you'll finish the task together.
D. Do your best, and you will pass the test.
E. Excellence opens doors to greater responsibilities.
F. Face your problems and work them out.
G. Goals require focus, planning, and direction.
H. Have respect and people will respect you.
I. Ignore those who try to mislead you into bad choices.
J. Join others in promoting understanding and peace.
K. Keep high expectations, and you will go far.
L. Those who give up miss out on life's best rewards.
M. Make yourself an honorable person.

N. Noteworthy people never neglect their responsibilities.

O. Remove negative thoughts from your mind and anger from your heart.

P. Parents, have you listened to your children lately?

Q. Stop disrupting class; act responsibly.

R. Correct the wise, and they will thank you.

S. A positive attitude makes a superior scholar.

T. Teamwork is cooperation at its best.

U. Education frees you from the grip of poverty.

V. Choose freedom, and you will live freely.

W. Wasting time is like wasting money.

X. Cross out negativity and let goodness in.

Y. Always strive to be your best.

Z. Erase bad habits from your life.

PROVERBS ARE THE JOURNEY OF LIFE

APPLY YOUR SKILLS FOR WHAT YOU LEARNED!

APPLY YOUR SKILLS FOR WHAT YOU LEARNED!

APPLY YOUR SKILLS OF WHAT YOU LEARNED!

15 September 2000

A. Apply what you've learned and keep building your skills.

B. Avoid harm and take care of your health.

C. Carefully plan your daily activities with thought and intention.

D. Do your homework and turn it in on time.

E. Expect yourself to be a role model.

F. Forgiveness is the only path to complete healing.

G. Give me your hand, and together, we can find peace.

H. Show respect for yourself and others.

I. Impatience won't get you where you're going any faster.

J. Just do the right thing, and you'll sleep soundly.

K. Keep yourself engaged to ward off boredom.

L. Love yourself so you can love the world around you.

M. Honor your promises.

N. Nothing should stop you from doing what's right.

O. Opportunities don't come often—seize them when they do.

P. Perseverance, persistence, and practice lead to success.

Q. Quit saying, "I can't."

R. Respect is your honorable road to serving others.

S. Serve those who strive to help themselves.

T. Tension causes headaches and stress—find ways to relax.

U. Understand your mistakes and correct them.

V. Variety of activities can break up the monotony.

W. Wealth isn't everything in life.

X. X-ray the future with clear vision.

Y. You oversee your own destiny and goals.

Z. Zigzag, you're on your way out of trouble with creativity.

ALLOW GOODNESS TO BRIGHTEN YOUR LIFE

ALLOW GOODNESS TO BRIGHTEN YOUR LIFE

JOHN A. SHALHOUB

ALLOW GOODNESS TO BRIGHTEN YOUR LIFE

15 September 2000

A. Allow goodness to grow in your heart.
B. Behavior reflects your inner soul.
C. Calm down and concentrate on your work.
D. Don't pretend to be something you're not.
E. Even when you don't know, make a thoughtful guess.
F. Face life with courage and you will be happier.
G. Great things don't come easily.
H. Have a healthy body and you will have a healthy mind.
I. Improve your attitude to shape your behavior.
J. Just be humble and true to yourself.
K. Keep your nose out of others' business.

PROVERBS ARE THE JOURNEY OF LIFE

L. Learn from history; otherwise, you risk repeating the same mistakes.

M. Mind your own business; don't interfere in others' affairs.

N. New experiences bring excitement and thrill.

O. Observe wisdom and learn from experience.

P. Practice consistently to improve your skills.

Q. Quiet down; avoid being loud.

R. Remember your manners and be kind to others.

S. Serve good causes and people will love you.

T. Take risks and chances; eventually, you will succeed.

U. Understand your intentions before you speak or act.

V. Victory smells like roses.

W. Work hard and support others so they can help you in return.

X. X failure from your achievement book,

Y. You love to shine when you do well!

Z. Zero has no value on the left of one.

ANSWER WHEN ASKED a QUESTION

ANSWER WHEN ASKED a QUESTION

ANSWER WHEN ASKED A QUESTION

3 October 20

A. Answer when asked and speak when needed.

B. Just as bees work to make honey, you need to work to earn money.

C. Cooperation is key to success.

D. Do your best both in school and at home.

E. Endure hardships, and you'll become stronger.

F. Steer away from evil and be peace-loving.

G. Give your best effort every day.

H. A healthy body comes from a balanced diet and lifestyle.

I. Ignore violence and welcome peace.

J. Do what is right and walk away from what is wrong.

K. Know that you can make a difference in your own life.

L. Love yourself, and you'll find it easier to love others.

M. Manage your life with care and wisdom.

N. Navigate the world with diligence.

O. Obey the truth, and you'll live in peace.

P. Peace should be everyone's goal.

Q. Quell your anger with love and forgiveness.

R. Remember, what goes up must come down.

S. Leave behind harmful ways and listen to your conscience.

T. Train your mind to do good.

U. Understand that doing the right thing is always worthwhile.

V. Reflect on your actions and stay responsible.

W. Watch your steps; know where you're going.

X. X is just a letter, but faith is hope.

Y. Embrace who you truly are.

Z. A "Z" may twist, but your mind should stay steady.

JOHN A. SHALHOUB

AMEND YOUR CROOKED WAYS AND BE RESPECTABLE!

AMEND YOUR CROOKED WAYS AND BE RESPECTABLE!

PROVERBS ARE THE JOURNEY OF LIFE

AMEND YOUR CROOKED WAYS AND BE RESPECTABLE

10 October 2005

A. Amend your crooked ways and do the right thing.
B. Be a peacemaker.
C. Conserve your energies and use them wisely.
D. Do your homework as soon as you get home.
E. Earn good grades, and that is your reward.
F. Follow instructions and pay attention.
G. Give respect to adults and listen to their advice.
H. Have an inquisitive mind, and you will find answers.
I. Inside your heart, you will find the truth.
J. Judge your work by the results you get.
K. Keep your thoughts in check.

L. Listen to your teachers and understand what they say.

M. Meet your obligations without hesitation.

N. Neglect your studies, and you will fail.

O. Outstanding performance is your prize.

P. Pass your test with honor and pride.

Q. Quit being a pest in class.

R. Resist evil and embrace godliness.

S. Share your skills with friends and be proud of yourself.

T. Treat others the way you want to be treated.

U. Use kind words and hear nice words.

V. View your future with clear binoculars.

W. Will you join me to work together?

X. X-ray your mind and choose the good thoughts.

Y. You should listen to the voice of your conscience.

Z. Z is for zero trouble in school.

PROVERBS ARE THE JOURNEY OF LIFE

DO NOT APPEASE A BULLY!

DO NOT APPEASE A BULLY!

JOHN A. SHALHOUB

DO NOT APPEASE A BULLY!

13 September 2008

A. Appease a bully, and he will continue to oppress you.

B. Be respectful to your elders, and they will praise you.

C. Cooperate with others to get the work done.

D. Do the right thing for yourself.

E. Examine your options and choose the best one.

F. Fair is fair when you try to be fair.

G. Good children don't disappoint their parents.

H. Helping others is always the right thing to do.

I. It's what's on the inside that counts.

J. Joking around too much will make you look like a clown.

K. Killing is against God's commandment.

L. Love is the key to a peaceful world.

M. Money is the root of evil, but it grows in the heart of man.

N. No secret will remain hidden forever.

O. Opportunity doesn't knock that often.

- **P.** Peace, peace, peace—seek peace and you will live in peace.
- **Q.** Questions are powerful tools for learning.
- **R.** Reading and writing are essential skills.
- **S.** Steady effort will improve your performance.
- **T.** Tomorrow is for tomorrow; today is for today.
- **U.** Unto you is given the fulfillment of your dreams.
- **V.** Vow to make your parents proud of you.
- **W.** When you go to bed, remember to have positive thoughts.
- **X.** X-ray your heart to know if you're truly okay.
- **Y.** You should be kind to others, even when it's difficult.
- **Z.** Zero in on your thoughts and be creative.

JOHN A. SHALHOUB

ACT RESPONSIBLY IN WHATEVER YOU DO!

ACT RESPONSIBLY IN WHATEVER YOU DO!

PROVERBS ARE THE JOURNEY OF LIFE

ACT RESPONSIBLY IN WHATEVER YOU DO!

21 March 2002

A. Act responsibly, and you will earn respect.

B. Build up your spirit, and don't get discouraged.

C. Compete for excellence.

D. Do the right thing to hear kind words.

E. Earn good grades, and be proud of yourself.

F. Face challenges with courage and pride.

G. Greet people with a friendly smile.

H. Happiness is the soft nest of the heart.

I. Ignore those who try to steer you in the wrong direction.

J. Joy is a song that flirts with your heart.

K. Keep up the good work.

L. Learn from those who are willing to teach you.

M. Make wise plans, and reap fruitful rewards.

N. Never give up control of your ship to strangers.

O. Open new doors to the future.

P. Practice makes determined, perfect heroes.

Q. Quick temper brings wrath; patience brings peace.

R. Responsibility grows with honesty.

S. Stay the course and reach your objective.

T. Take your time and do good work.

U. Uniformity gives a false sense of security.

V. Vow never to use drugs or alcohol.

W. Watch your actions and stay out of trouble.

X. X out the bad things from your life.

Y. You should make the right choices for your life.

Z. Zero tolerance for violence makes a peaceful world.

PROVERBS ARE THE JOURNEY OF LIFE

APPRECIATE WHAT YOU HAVE OF BLESSING

APPRECIATE WHAT YOU HAVE OF BLESSING

APPRECIATE WHAT YOU HAVE OF BLESSING

21 March 1996

A. Appreciate what you have and avoid selfishness.

B. Be kind to others, and they will be kind to you.

C. Care for others, and practice selflessness.

D. Do your homework to improve your grades.

E. Embrace the truth, and let joy fill your heart.

F. Fairness reduces jealousy and fills the heart with joy.

G. It's great to feel good—especially when things go your way.

H. Heart is the organ that gives your life.

I. Improve your lifestyle to reduce tension.

J. Just be kind and friendly to classmates.

PROVERBS ARE THE JOURNEY OF LIFE

K. Knock, and the door will open to you.

L. Look, those who don't give up get ahead in life.

M. Money can be rooted in good rather than evil.

N. Noble causes have noble champions.

O. Oust fear from your heart.

P. Please, don't be obnoxious or vicious; just be kind.

Q. Quit being a pest.

R. Respect everyone, and they will respect you.

S. Smile, and the world will smile with you.

T. Trouble is something you don't need.

U. Understand the conversation.

V. View the future with a positive attitude.

W. Wash your hands before and after you eat.

X. X-out failure from your life.

Y. You oversee your own life.

Z. Zoom in on the good things in life.

PROVERBS ARE THE JOURNEY OF LIFE

ACHIEVE YOUR GOALS WITH PRIDE!

ACHIEVE YOUR GOALS WITH PRIDE!

JOHN A. SHALHOUB

ACHIEVE YOUR GOALS WITH PRIDE

2 December 2004

A. Achieve your goals, and finish what you start.

B. Broaden your mind and treat others fairly.

C. Control your temper and conquer your anger.

D. Do your work now; don't put off for tomorrow what you can do today.

E. Experience is irreplaceable—learn from it.

F. Follow your dreams until they're real.

G. Good deeds bring recognition and respect.

H. Honor your responsibilities wholeheartedly.

I. Ignore foolishness and use common sense.

J. Just give your best effort—you'll be okay.

K. Kindness is a gift; be thoughtful and compassionate.

L. Learn to respect others, and they will respect you.

PROVERBS ARE THE JOURNEY OF LIFE

M. Memorize life's sacred rules: respect and honesty.

N. Never do drugs—especially the hard stuff.

O. Only the pure in heart find peace of mind.

P. Pass on the bad and pursue the good in life.

Q. Quit being lazy and do better work to succeed.

R. Respect and integrity will bring you honor.

S. Self-discipline strengthens both mind and body.

T. Take responsibility for all your actions.

U. Understand your goals and proceed with care.

V. Vacant mind contributes nothing—fill it with knowledge.

W. Wear the truth and let it guide your words.

X. X-ray your mind and learn about yourself.

Y. You are unique—embrace it!

Z. Zeros in life hold you back; aim higher.

JOHN A. SHALHOUB

ALLEVIATE YOUR PAIN AND BE HEALTHY!

ALLEVIATE YOUR PAIN AND BE HEALTHY!

PROVERBS ARE THE JOURNEY OF LIFE

ALLEVIATE YOUR PAIN AND BE HEALTHY!

1 September 1994

A. Alleviate pain and suffering from your life.

B. Be responsible and live up to your promises.

C. Care for your family and be honest with them.

D. Don't give up on yourself; give it your all.

E. Everyone deserves an opportunity.

F. Forgive others; don't seek retaliation.

G. Give support to others, and they'll be grateful.

H. Help people when they ask for it.

I. Inspiration leads you to wonderful dreams.

J. Just do the best you can!

K. Know your opponent; never underestimate anyone.

- **L.** Lying is distasteful, and stealing is repulsive.
- **M.** Master your studies and aim for good grades.
- **N.** No pain, no gain; just keep doing the right thing.
- **O.** Open your heart and mind to the truth.
- **P.** Preparedness helps you avoid unpleasant surprises.
- **Q.** Quit talking and take time to listen.
- **R.** Review your actions and steer clear of wrong turns.
- **S.** Scrutinize the facts before reaching conclusions.
- **T.** Trust yourself, even when things go wrong.
- **U.** Use good manners and respect others' views.
- **V.** View the world with a realistic perspective.
- **W.** Wheel of victory turns with caution and diligence.
- **X.** X out negative influences from your life.

PROVERBS ARE THE JOURNEY OF LIFE

Y. Yield the control of your life to sound thinking.

Z. Zero yourself from the mess you create.

JOHN A. SHALHOUB

APPROACH LIFE WITH VIGOR AND CAUTION

APPROACH LIFE WITH VIGOR AND CAUTION

PROVERBS ARE THE JOURNEY OF LIFE

APPROACH LIFE WITH VIGOR WITH CAUTION

15 May 2004

A. 11 September 2003 Approach life with caution and a strong vision.

B. Books are loyal friends; they won't betray you.

C. Citizenship means being responsible for each other's welfare.

D. Don't make poor choices; avoid the wrong crowd.

E. Endure life's hardships with patience.

F. Failure should not be an option.

G. Grow your interests to keep improving.

H. Helplessness is not part of a strong character.

I. Ignorance leads only to more ignorance.

J. Joking doesn't provide true security in life.

K. Keep your promises and honor your commitments.

L. Lying and gossiping bring harm to you and others.

M. Manage your life diligently.

N. Never say never; always be prepared to do your best.

O. Outstanding students always shine.

P. Participate actively in class discussions.

Q. Question yourself whenever you have doubts.

R. Respect yourself, and others will respect you too.

S. Solve your problems and avoid burdening others.

T. Train yourself to recognize the truth.

U. Understand how others think and feel.

V. Violate no rules and avoid unnecessary fines.

W. Respect others' property and foster goodwill.

X. X-out bad habits from your life.

Y. You can become whatever you aspire to be.

Z. Zero adds no value on the left, but aim for a perfect score.

JOHN A. SHALHOUB

ATTEND SCHOOL FAITHFULLY

ATTEND SCHOOL FAITHFULLY

ATTEND SCHOOL FAITHFULLY

By

Dr. Fr. John Shalhoub

15 September 2003

A. Attend school faithfully to advance and succeed.

B. Believe in yourself, and always put in your best effort.

C. Check your work thoroughly before turning it in.

D. Demand the best from yourself to reach your goals.

E. Encourage yourself to keep climbing the ladder of success.

F. Focus on your goals and work diligently to achieve them.

G. Give your best in everything you do.

H. Have faith in yourself; patience will come with time.

I. Inspiration provides the spark to start anew.

J. Judge only yourself; let go of judging others.

K. Keep your mind focused and your body healthy.

L. Leap confidently into the future to make your dreams real.

M. Manage your life with diligence and care.

N. Never compromise your values or character.

O. Obstacles are steps—use them to reach higher ground.

P. Practice makes progress; keep learning new skills.

Q. Quality of life comes from doing what's right at every step.

R. Respect others, and they will respect you.

S. Study with the purpose to become your best.

T. Take pride in your work and aim for excellence.

U. Utilize your time wisely—make every moment count.

V. Value your education and take it seriously.

PROVERBS ARE THE JOURNEY OF LIFE

W. Wise decisions create a wise life.

X. X-ray your future and set goals that fulfill your dreams.

Y. You can be anything—choose wisely.

Z. Zap through your homework with focus and determination.

JOHN A. SHALHOUB

ACCEPT RESPONSIBILITY WITH HUMILITY

ACCEPT RESPONSIBILITY WITH HUMILITY

ACCEPT RESPONSIBILITY WITH HUMILITY

11 September 2003

A. Accept responsibility for your actions.
B. Be kind and respectful to others, and they'll do the same.
C. Care for others without being judgmental.
D. Do your homework and turn it in on time.
E. Expect success, not defeat.
F. Forget your flaws, but learn from your mistakes.
G. Go after your goals with all your energy.
H. Honor your father and mother.
I. Inspiration can kindle your spirit.
J. Just keep climbing; reach for the stars.
K. Kindle your life with hope.
L. Live with love, virtue, and care for others.
M. Make good grades and be a proud student.

N. Nothing should dampen your spirit.
O. Opportunities don't knock often; be ready.
P. Persuasion, not fighting, is the path to peace.
Q. Quit bad habits and develop good ones.
R. Respect others, and they will respect you.
S. Success should be your goal.
T. Tension breeds anger; try to relax.
U. Understand your mistakes and learn from them.
V. Volunteer your time to help others.
W. Wealth isn't everything in life, but honesty is.
X. X-out the bad and choose the good.
Y. You are perfect in your own way.
Z. Zap into a world of peace and find joy.

PROVERBS ARE THE JOURNEY OF LIFE

APOLOGIZE FOR YOU HURT SOMEONE!

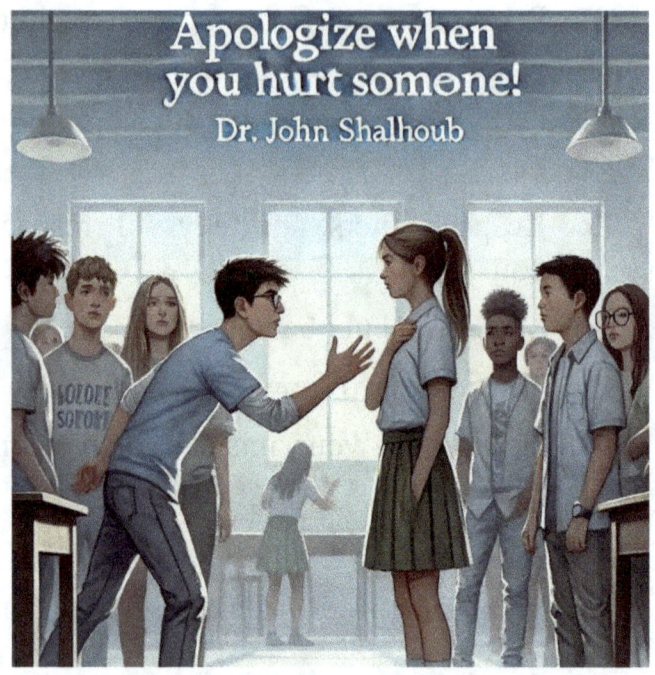

APOLOGIZE FOR YOU HURT SOMEONE!

APOLOGIZE FOR HURTING SOMEONE!

14 September 2004

- **A.** Apologize sincerely when you hurt someone.
- **B.** Be your best in knowledge and integrity.
- **C.** Change negative habits and live righteously.
- **D.** Don't multitask excessively; focus on one thing at a time.
- **E.** Excellence is essential to success.
- **F.** Friendships should be valued deeply.
- **G.** Goals and dreams shape your future.
- **H.** Have a genuine, healthy attitude.
- **I.** Investigate, anticipate, and stay in control.
- **J.** Judge no one and harm no one.
- **K.** Keep trying until you succeed.
- **L.** Love yourself so you can love others around you.
- **M.** Move thoughtfully, respecting others' space.

- **N.** Never judge anyone by their appearance.
- **O.** Open your heart to honesty and freedom.
- **P.** Peace is a shared dream for all humanity.
- **Q.** Quietness in class helps everyone learn.
- **R.** Reach for the stars and aim to shine.
- **S.** Silence can lead to self-discovery.
- **T.** Teach others the knowledge they need.
- **U.** Use your mind wisely and take care of your health.
- **V.** Violence never justifies violence.
- **W.** Watch your steps and tread carefully.
- **X.** X out assignments after completing them.
- **Y.** Your first responsibility is to yourself.
- **Z.** Zip your lips when elders are speaking.

JOHN A. SHALHOUB

ALWAYS STUDY IN ORDER TO SUCCEED!

ALWAYS STUDY IN ORDER TO SUCCEED!

PROVERBS ARE THE JOURNEY OF LIFE

ALWAYS STUDY IN ORDER TO SUCCEED!

10 September 2004

A. Always study and use your time wisely.

B. Be a dedicated student and focus on your education.

C. Carelessness leads to problems; organization leads to solutions.

D. Do your homework and submit it on time.

E. Exams help reveal how much you've learned.

F. Fighting fuels conflict, but peace creates harmony.

G. Good students complete their work on time.

H. Have faith in yourself, and don't give up.

I. Integrate kindness and grace into your character.

J. Junk food can harm your body.

K. Kick bad habits and develop a strong work ethic.

L. Lying is harmful, but the truth sets you free.

M. Make good grades and shine as a star student.

N. Neglect no one and be kind to all.

O. Oppose violence and support peace and harmony.

P. "Please" is a powerful word for building good relationships.

Q. Quit pestering others and focus on your own growth.

R. Responsibility is essential and should never be ignored.

S. Study hard for a report card you're proud of.

T. Try your best to be among the best.

U. Understand your responsibilities and commitments.

V. Vacations are valuable for relaxation with family.

W. Weekends are for relaxation and recharging.

X.   X has endless applications in math and science.

Y.   Yield to the truth, and it will guide your life.

Z.   Zip through your homework and finish on time.

JOHN A. SHALHOUB

ATTITUDE COUNTS

ATTITUDE COUNTS

PROVERBS ARE THE JOURNEY OF LIFE

ATTITUDE COUNTS

19 August 2000

A. Attitude matters, and so do you.

B. Be a responsible citizen; do your part.

C. Character is key to shaping your personality.

D. Avoid illegal drugs—they can harm you.

E. Expand your mind with quality education.

F. Finding the truth starts with telling the truth.

G. Giving is as rewarding as receiving.

H. Helping others can lead to new friendships.

I. It's important to do the right thing.

J. Junk food isn't good for you—limit it.

K. Keep your grades up and stay positive.

L. Learn new skills to build a fulfilling life.

M. Meet new students and make new friends.

N. Noble people pursue noble causes.

O. Obedience often earns respect.

P. People deserve respect, whoever they are.

Q. Quick, smart thinking can be a lifesaver.

R. Rule #1: Believe in yourself.

S. Some people may use drugs, but you don't have to.

T. Tutoring can help strengthen your skills.

U. Use your time wisely; don't waste it.

V. Variety in life experiences enriches your perspective.

W. Watch your grades improve and feel the reward.

X. X-out bad choices and aim for the good ones.

Y. You can achieve it if you believe you can.

Z. Zip up your lips, focus, and get to work.

PROVERBS ARE THE JOURNEY OF LIFE

STAY FOCUSED ON YOUR WORK!

STAY FOCUSED ON YOUR WORK!

JOHN A. SHALHOUB

STAY FOCUSED ON YOUR WORK!

20 August 2004

A. Always focus on your work to succeed.

B. Be kind to others, and they may do the same.

C. Caution can spare you a lot of pain and regret.

D. Don't do drugs—they can burn your life away.

E. Education and good manners are always worth it.

F. Fight for the truth; avoid anger and aggression.

G. Good behavior shows respect and dignity.

H. Help your community family, and obey the law.

I. Inspiration fuels discipline and creativity.

J. Justice should apply equally to all.

PROVERBS ARE THE JOURNEY OF LIFE

K. Keep away from illegal drugs.

L. Listen to your parents and show them kindness.

M. Make your family and friends proud of you.

N. "No" is a complete answer when offered drugs.

O. Outstanding effort earns outstanding results.

P. Prepare your work carefully; don't waste time.

Q. Quit fooling around and listen to your parents.

R. Read today, and you'll thank yourself tomorrow.

S. Save time and money to avoid hunger later.

T. Trust yourself when in doubt.

U. Understand yourself to make wise choices.

V. Victory is reaching your goals.

W. Wisdom is showing respect and good manners.

X. X marks completed work—check things off!

Y. You are a trustworthy person.

Z. Zoom to the stars and find yours.

A GOOD PERSON DOES NOT HARM OTHERS

A GOOD PERSON DOES NOT HARM OTHERS

JOHN A. SHALHOUB

A GOOD PERSON DOES NOT HARM OTHERS

14 November 2004

A. A good person is a responsible one.

B. Be responsible and keep your promises.

C. Call for help when you're in need.

D. Don't do drugs; they're dangerous.

E. Eat healthy food to stay strong and fit.

F. Food fuels your mind and body, keeping you smart and healthy.

G. Get good grades, and you'll earn praise.

H. Help others whenever you can.

I. I offer help when people call on me.

J. Just listen to your parents and teachers.

K. Keep drugs and trouble out of your home.

L. Let's eat healthy and live well.

M. Make your family proud of your achievements.

N. Never try drugs; just say "No."

O. Obedience outshines rebellion.

PROVERBS ARE THE JOURNEY OF LIFE

P. Preparation is the key to success.

Q. Quit disruptive behavior at home and school.

R. Responsible people make great citizens.

S. Some people are truly worthy of trust.

T. Trouble can ruin your life—choose peace.

U. Use your time wisely; every minute counts.

V. Villains make bad citizens. Be good!

W. When you allow yourself to make bad choices, you risk becoming bad.

X. Examine your goals and make wise choices.

Y. You steer your own ship—choose the right course.

Z. Zero isn't an option; aim higher.

JOHN A. SHALHOUB

APPLY YOUR SKILLS IN YOUR STUDIES

APPLY YOUR SKILLS IN YOUR STUDIES

PROVERBS ARE THE JOURNEY OF LIFE

APPLY YOUR SKILLS IN YOUR STUDIES

22 August 2002

A. Apply your skills and experience wisely.
B. Be a star; shine in all that you do.
C. Character is #1—cultivate it.
D. The dictionary is your best friend in school.
E. Education is the portion you carve for yourself.
F. Follow directions and listen to your conscience.
G. Forgive, and you will be forgiven.
H. Have a loving heart, and you'll attract warm friends.
I. Good grades pave the way to graduation.
J. Justice, love, and compassion are for everyone.
K. Keep sharp objects away from your eyes (and other important places).
L. Love is your road to peace and harmony.
M. Live up to your responsibilities.
N. Now is the time to pay attention.
O. Obey your parents and your conscience.
P. Protect yourself from drugs.
Q. Quit talking when the teacher is speaking.
R. Respect human life and all living things.

- **S.** Select only what you need—don't be wasteful.
- **T.** Teachers are here to guide you, so listen.
- **U.** Use your ears more in class and your mouth less.
- **V.** Violence has no place in school—avoid it.
- **W.** Strive to win but learn along the way.
- **X.** Out drugs—don't let them take hold.
- **Y.** Know what to do next.
- **Z.** Zip your lips and open your mind.

EXCELLENCE IS EXCELLENCE

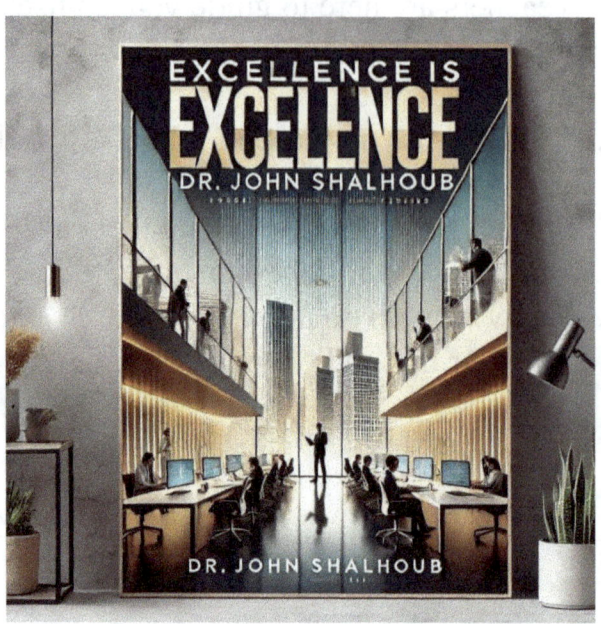

EXCELLENCE IS EXCELLENCE

JOHN A. SHALHOUB

EXCELLENCE IS EXCELLENCE

21 August 2006

A. A is an A; it will put you in the
B. Be careful with strangers; don't gamble with your life.
C. Care for your family and friends.
D. Discipline yourself and organize your daily activities.
E. Expectations can keep you focused on the right path.
F. Fight for your rights.
G. God and Goodness furnish courage and patience.
H. Have good manners, even when alone.
I. Initiative will open doors to new places.
J. Join the right people; avoid corruption.
K. Keep up the good work.
L. Leave trouble alone; steer clear of violence.
M. Make a good report card and earn praise.
N. Never say no to learning.

PROVERBS ARE THE JOURNEY OF LIFE

O. Open your mind to new knowledge and skills.

P. People will like you if you're kind.

Q. Quit being a clown or seeking attention.

R. Respect your family and friends.

S. Study hard, and good grades will follow.

T. Teach kids good manners and respect.

U. Understand your choices and make wise ones.

V. Violence only leads to more violence.

W. Work hard to reach your goals.

X. X-ray your mind; choose the right path.

Y. You can be all you dream to be.

Z. Zoo is for animals; the classroom is for students.

JOHN A. SHALHOUB

ALWAYS BE KIND AND FRIENDLY TO OTHERS

ALWAYS BE KIND AND FRIENDLY TO OTHERS

PROVERBS ARE THE JOURNEY OF LIFE

ALWAYS BE KIND AND FRIENDLY TO OTHERS

A. Always treat others with kindness and fairness.

B. Be your best self, with integrity and honesty.

C. Chase your dreams and create your own success.

D. Depend on yourself—self-reliance leads to achievement.

E. Everyone has the power to bring fresh ideas.

F. Funny things can sometimes hurt; laugh thoughtfully.

G. Goodness brings comfort to the heart.

H. Hate corrodes the spirit, like rust on metal.

I. Inspire yourself to succeed by doing your best.

J. Jealousy poisons the soul—replace it with gratitude.

K. Kindness nourishes the soul like love fills the heart.

L. Love your family, friends, and the people around you.

M. Make others happy, and respect will follow.

N. Never support evil or condone violence.

O. Oppose negativity and surround yourself with positivity.

P. Peace on earth begins with shared dreams and actions.

Q. Quality of life is a right we all deserve.

R. Respect is golden; it brings harmony to everyone.

S. Study diligently, and success will follow.

T. Take part in your community; lead by example.

U. Use your time wisely; make every moment count.

V. Volunteer to help others—it's a gift to them and you.

W. Waiting patiently often brings the best rewards.

PROVERBS ARE THE JOURNEY OF LIFE

X. X-mas reminds us to hope for a brighter world.

Y. You shine brightest when you stay true to yourself.

Z. Zoom past trouble; don't let it slow you down.

JOHN A. SHALHOUB

THE DOOR IS OPEN FOR BETTER FUTURE!

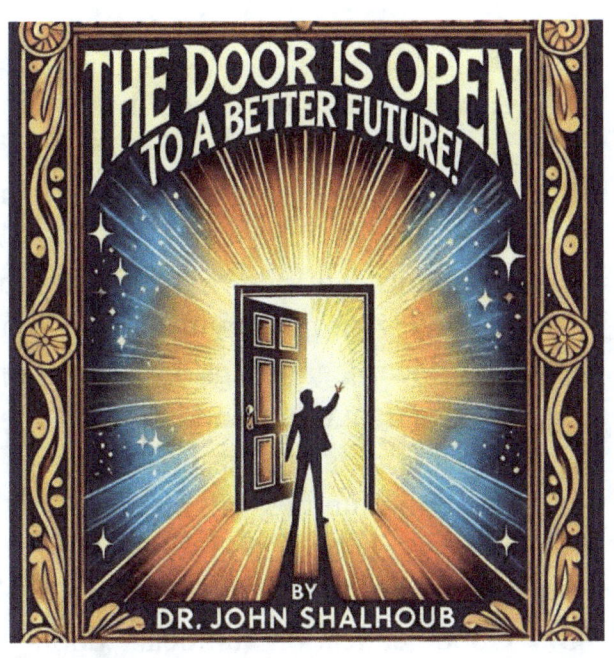

THE DOOR IS OPEN FOR BETTER FUTURE!

PROVERBS ARE THE JOURNEY OF LIFE

THE DOOR IS OPEN FOR BETTER FUTURE!

21 August 2007

A. Always strive for quality in your work—it defines your character.
B. Be smart, stay ambitious, and avoid laziness.
C. Continue working hard, and you'll achieve your goals with satisfaction.
D. Don't let illegal drugs derail your life; they're dangerous and harmful.
E. Education is a treasure—pursue it, and opportunities will come.
F. Food fuels both body and mind; eat well to nurture them.
G. Good education unlocks doors to rewarding jobs.
H. Honesty lights the clearest path to truth.
I. Inspire others by caring for them as they care for you.
J. Justice means living truthfully and helping others do the same.
K. Keep your space clean to avoid unnecessary chaos (and pests!).
L. Live honestly to enjoy peace of mind.

M. Manners are your way of showing respect to others.
N. Never surrender to challenges—persistence is the key to success.
O. Overcome negativity by opposing what brings you down.
P. Promote peace—it's the foundation of a fulfilling life.
Q. Quit distractions when it's time to focus on your goals. R. Responsibility means owning your actions and learning from them.
S. Share your knowledge and skills to uplift others.
T. Talk through your problems to find peaceful solutions.
U. Understand and respect your own needs to thrive.
V. Verify the truth before jumping to conclusions.
W. When you hurt someone, apologize sincerely—it heals wounds.
X. X is a letter of the Alphabet.
Y. You must trust yourself; confidence leads to achievement.
Z. Zeal drives effective leadership and inspires others.

ALWAYS APPRECIATE WHAT YOU CAN DO

ALWAYS APPRECIATE WHAT YOU CAN DO

JOHN A. SHALHOUB

ALWAYS APPRECIATE WHAT YOU CAN DO

21 August 2003

A. Appreciate what you can do for others.

B. Be responsible for your actions.

C. Cooperate with others to find answers to your questions.

D. Don't be late for school or appointments.

E. Explain your thoughts so others understand you.

F. Fairness is key; treat others fairly to receive fairness in return.

G. Go for what's right; avoid what's wrong.

H. Have integrity, and people will trust you.

I. Improve your attitude, and you'll make more friends.

J. Junk food is junk for your body.

K. Keep busy with your schoolwork.

L. Love and be kind to others.

M. Make good decisions to build confidence.

PROVERBS ARE THE JOURNEY OF LIFE

N. Never be mean to friends.

O. Obey the law and respect authority.

P. Pack your bag with schoolbooks the night before.

Q. Quit causing trouble or acting out.

R. Respect earns respect; anger invites anger.

S. Stay busy to ease anxiety.

T. Tolerate others' differences.

U. Use your time wisely and save your money.

V. Visit community events and meet people.

W. Write neatly and keep things organized.

X. X-mas celebrates the birth of Jesus.

Y. You and I are a team—we work better together.

Z. Zip your lips when tempted to say something unkind.

JOHN A. SHALHOUB

ADMINISTER YOUR CHORES DILIGENTLY

ADMINISTER YOUR CHORES DILIGENTLY

PROVERBS ARE THE JOURNEY OF LIFE

ADMINISTER YOUR CHORES DILIGENTLY

21 August 2024

A. Administer your daily chores with care.

B. Be always ready and prepared in everything you do.

C. Citizenship means loving and being loyal to your country.

D. Do your chores and strive to do the right thing.

E. Eat right to live well.

F. Fighting leads to more violence, but peace brings joy.

G. Give generously, and you will feel fulfilled.

H. Have self-confidence and trust yourself.

I. Inspiration will encourage you to pursue better things in life.

J. Just do the right thing; don't only ask, "What's in it for me?"

K. Keep up the good work.

L. Littering and loitering are unacceptable.

M. Mom and Dad want the best for you.

N. No cussing or profanity is allowed anywhere.

O. Oppose violence and seek peace.

P. Prepare thoroughly for your tests and exams.

Q. Quit being disruptive in the classroom.

R. Remove distractions that hinder your studies.

S. See what you can do to help the less fortunate.

T. Teamwork teaches you to care and share.

U. Use your time wisely; focus on your schoolwork.

V. Violence should not be tolerated anywhere.

PROVERBS ARE THE JOURNEY OF LIFE

W. Write your homework neatly.

X. Expect loyalty from your friends, and don't leave them behind.

Y. Your honesty defines your truthfulness.

Z. Zealous ambition will guide you to success.

JOHN A. SHALHOUB

ACHIEVE YOUR GOALS FROM A to Z

ACHIEVE YOUR GOALS FROM A to Z

PROVERBS ARE THE JOURNEY OF LIFE

ACHIEVE YOUR GOALS FROM A TO Z

By

Father John Shalhoub

12 June 2005

A. **Achieve** your goals and do a good work.

B. **Be nice** to your family and friends

C. **Concentrate** on your goals and do not give up.

D. **Do your best** and that is the best.

E. **Earn good reports** and you will make yourself and your family proud.

F. **Figure out** your dilemmas and solve them.

G. **God is** the origin of all the universe.

H. **Have good manners** and everyone will respect you.

I. **Improve your attitude** and be a humble person.

J. **Jealousy** is a deadly poison for your life.

K. **Kindness** is food for your spirit.

L. **Lying** will corrode your life.

M. **Make sure** to keep your room and home neat.

N. **Never call people bad names** or be sarcastic about them.

O. **Obey your coaches**, supervisors, and parents.

P. Practice and don't give up, and you will succeed .QQ.**Quit being a clown** around; be a loving person.

R. **Respect others** and they will respect you.

S. **Study every night** and complete your assigned work.

T. **Try your best** and you become one of the best.

U. **Use your best behavior** wherever you are.

V. **Victory** is what you need for yourself.

W. **Work hard** and you will be successful in your life.

X. **X is a check mark** before the completed task.

Y. **You must try your best** to be one of the best.

JOHN A. SHALHOUB

ABC INSTRUCTIONS FOR A BETTER LIFE

ABC INSTRUCTIONS FOR A BETTER LIFE

PROVERBS ARE THE JOURNEY OF LIFE

ABC INSTRUCTIONS FOR A BETTER LIFE

25 February 2013

A. Answer when asked and speak only when it truly matters.

B. Bees work tirelessly to make honey; you must work diligently to earn your success.

C. Cooperation is the key to achieving lasting success.

D. Do your best in everything, striving for excellence where no one else can surpass you.

E. Endure hardships, for they shape you into a stronger and better person.

F. Flee from evil and embrace a life of peace and kindness. Give your best effort every day, no matter the circumstances.

H. Healthy body requires a disciplined lifestyle and a nutritious diet.

I. Ignore violence and open your heart to peace and understanding.

J. Just do what is right and walk away from what you know is wrong.

K. Know that you have the power to change your life for the better.
L. Love yourself first, for it allows you to love others fully.
M. Manage your life with care, wisdom, and intentionality.
N. Navigate through life with diligence and a clear sense of purpose.
O. Obey the truth, and you will find peace within yourself.
P. Peace should be the shared hope and goal of every individual.
Q. Quell your anger with love, forgiveness, and understanding.
R. Remember, what goes up must come down; stay grounded.
S. Stop harmful ways and listen to the guiding voice of your conscience.
T. Train your mind to focus on goodness and the right actions. U. Understand that doing the right thing is always worthwhile.
V. Reflect on your thoughts, and take responsibility for your actions.
W. Watch your steps carefully and be mindful of the path you take.

X. X marks an unknown, but faith illuminates the truth and goodness of life.
Y. You must embrace and love yourself for who you truly are.
Z. Z may twist and turn, but keep your mind clear and your vision focused.

JOHN A. SHALHOUB

ADMIRING ROLE MODELS FOR GOOD BEHAVIOR

ADMIRING ROLE MODELS FOR GOOD BEHAVIOR

PROVERBS ARE THE JOURNEY OF LIFE

ADMIRING ROLE MODELS FOR GOOD BEHAVIOR

22 August 2024

A. Admire role models who guide you in the right direction.

B. Believe in yourself; don't let doubt hold you back.

C. Confess your mistakes and always tell the truth.

D. Don't initiate trouble; choose to walk away from hostility.

E. Everyone needs love and compassion.

F. Find a good friend, and you'll have a lifelong ally.

G. Good people create goodness through their actions.

H. Hate and forgiveness are both parts of life—choose forgiveness.

I. Initiate good deeds, and you'll never stand alone.

J. Justice thrives when honesty and truthfulness prevail.

K. Kick bad habits to the curb and choose to do what's right.

L. Lying tarnishes your mind and soul—stay truthful.

M. Making fair laws helps protect people from harm.

N. Never hate or belittle anyone.

O. Optimism fuels hope, success, and fulfillment.

P. Participate wholeheartedly to see the job through.

Q. Quiz yourself to ensure you've understood what you studied.

R. Respect others, and they'll respect you in return.

S. Share your wisdom and experiences to inspire others.

T. Tattling and gossip hurt more than they help—avoid both.

U. Unstable homes often create instability—strive to build peace.

V. Volunteer your time to help those in need.

PROVERBS ARE THE JOURNEY OF LIFE

W. Willingness is 90% of success!

X. X-marks symbolize excellence—strive for it!

Y. You can do it; never say, "I can't."

Z. Zoom in on good deeds, and you'll always feel fulfilled.

JOHN A. SHALHOUB

ATTITUDE AND HUMILITY ARE BASICS FOR GOOD FRIENDS.

ATTITUDE AND HUMILITY ARE BASICS FOR GOOD FRIENDS.

PROVERBS ARE THE JOURNEY OF LIFE

ATTITUDE AND HUMILITY ARE BASICS FOR GOOD FRIENDS.

14 September 2003

- **A.** Attitude is the key to good manners.
- **B.** Be friendly and kind to other students.
- **C.** Concentrate on your work and make the most of your time.
- **D.** Do your best, and you'll find happiness in the effort.
- **E.** Education is like money in the bank—an investment for your future.
- **F.** Friends are invaluable in times of need.
- **G.** A good citizen is a responsible person.
- **H.** Honesty is a quality everyone should cherish.
- **I.** Inflexibility can lead to destruction—stay open-minded.
- **J.** Jealousy corrodes the spirit just as rust corrodes metal.
- **K.** Keen students understand the value of time.

- **L.** Love and cherish your family and friends.
- **M.** Manipulate no one and treat others fairly.
- **N.** Never allow violence to cause pain or harm.
- **O.** Obey the law and avoid outsmarting yourself.
- **P.** Practice what you're good at and keep improving.
- **Q.** Quietness helps you focus and excel in class.
- **R.** Remember who you truly are and stay authentic.
- **S.** Stay on task and complete your work diligently.
- **T.** Trust your teachers and parents—they want the best for you.
- **U.** Use your mind wisely and your heart compassionately.
- **V.** Violence destroys, but love heals and unites.
- **W.** Work diligently and remain faithful to your goals.

PROVERBS ARE THE JOURNEY OF LIFE

X. X out bad habits and cultivate good ones.

Y. You must believe in yourself to achieve your dreams.

Z. Zip through your responsibilities with focus and enthusiasm.

JOHN A. SHALHOUB

ATTENTION TO DETAILS IN YOUR WORK

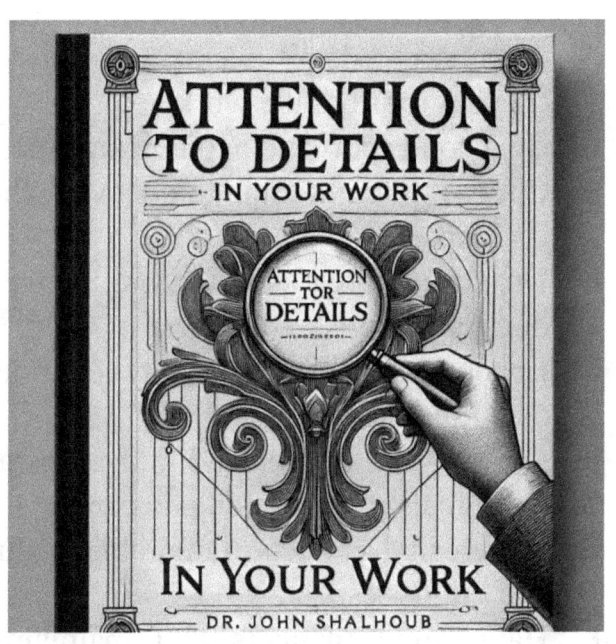

ATTENTION TO DETAILS IN YOUR WORK

PROVERBS ARE THE JOURNEY OF LIFE

ATTENTION TO DETAILS IN YOUR WORK
26 AUGUST 2005

A. Attention to detail is essential—always do your share of the work.
B. Be a good sport and avoid being a pest.
C. Choose the right thing to do, even when it's hard.
D. Do your chores and stay productive—don't be lazy.
E. Encourage yourself to stay confident and optimistic.
F. Form good habits and move toward your goals with caution and care.
G. Generosity reflects honorable values and builds respect.
H. Have good manners and maintain a positive attitude.
I. Integrity will earn you the trust and respect of others.
J. A joyful personality can attract many friends.
K. Keep up the good work to earn great grades and rewards.
L. Listen attentively, stay engaged, and provide feedback to your teacher.
M. Meet your responsibilities with commitment and pride.

N. Nice behavior is always noticed and appreciated.
O. Open doors for others, especially elders, as a sign of respect.
P. Please avoid smoking or using drugs—they harm your potential.
Q. Quit bullying and choose kindness instead—it's the better path.
R. Stand at attention and show respect when speaking to adults.
S. Stay aware of your surroundings—don't stumble through life!
T. Treat others the way you wish to be treated.
U. Use wisdom to improve your education, decisions, and manners.
V. Victory in school means earning good grades and growing as a person.
W. Wait patiently in line—complaining won't get you there faster.
X. X-ray your thoughts carefully and focus on the positive ones.
Y. You need to feel safe, secure, and like you belong—build this for others, too.
Z. Zero effort leads to zero results—strive for excellence!

ACT RIGHT AND FEEL RIGHT

ACT RIGHT AND FEEL RIGHT

JOHN A. SHALHOUB

ACT RIGHT AND FEEL RIGHT

26 August 2002

A. Act appropriately, and you will feel confident.

B. Believe in the truth, and you will find peace.

C. Concentrate on your studies, and you will succeed.

D. Divide your time wisely and plan your days effectively.

E. Explain yourself clearly to ensure understanding.

F. Force never justifies violence.

G. Give me your loyalty, and I will always stand by you.

H. Haughtiness leads to emptiness and arrogance.

I. Impress your classmates with honesty, and they will respect you.

J. Jealousy is like a cancer; it will consume you if you let it.

K. Kindness, love, and integrity are essential virtues.

PROVERBS ARE THE JOURNEY OF LIFE

L. Lying harms others and damages your own reputation.

M. Make sure to complete your homework diligently.

N. Nothing good comes from emptiness, but effort brings results.

O. Open the door to your future by planning wisely.

P. Please listen carefully when someone speaks to you.

Q. Quit flirting with danger; it could lead to harm.

R. Replenish your heart with love and your mind with knowledge.

S. A sound mind thrives in a sound body.

T. Take care of today; tomorrow will follow naturally.

U. Underneath it all, you are a unique and special person.

V. Victory is sweeter when earned through hard work.

W. When trouble comes, face it with honesty and courage.

X.   Examine your goals and pursue them with patience.

Y.   You should always correct your mistakes to grow.

Z.   Zero effort leads to zero results— always do your best.

PROVERBS ARE THE JOURNEY OF LIFE

ACCEPT YOUR PLACE OF HONOR

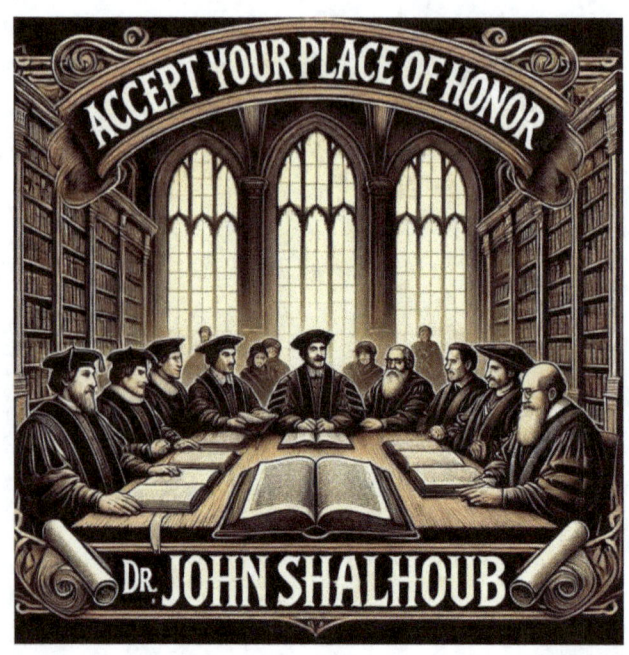

ACCEPT YOUR PLACE OF HONOR

JOHN A. SHALHOUB

ACCEPT YOUR PLACE OF HONOR

27 August 2003

A. Accept your place of honor with humility and integrity.

B. Behavior matters—improve it, and others will respect you.

C. Concentrate fully on your tasks and assignments.

D. Destroy nothing and harm no one.

E. Earn good grades to make your parents proud.

F. Figure out tough problems and tackle them with determination.

G. Give your best effort to overcome challenges.

H. Have good manners and common sense to gain respect.

I. Improve your attitude and count your blessings every day.

J. Jealousy and obsession cause unnecessary hardships.

PROVERBS ARE THE JOURNEY OF LIFE

K. Kindness is the cornerstone of true humility.

L. Lying erodes trust and damages relationships.

M. Make it a habit to submit your homework on time.

N. Nonsense leads to foolishness—stay focused and productive.

O. Obedience, when paired with intelligence, earns respect.

P. Practice consistently, and success will follow naturally.

Q. Quit any situation that promotes violence or harm.

R. Respond quickly and respectfully to instructions.

S. Stealing isolates you and makes you an outcast.

T. Turn over a new leaf and thrive like flowers in spring.

U. Use your best behavior to leave a positive impression.

V. Victory is achieved through hard work and contentment.

W. Work diligently to accomplish excellent results.

X. X on a checklist means the task is complete.

Y. You must strive daily to be your best self.

Z. Zero grades are painful—always give your best effort.

PROVERBS ARE THE JOURNEY OF LIFE

ACHIEVE YOUR GOALS WITH PRIDE

ACHIEVE YOUR GOALS WITH PRIDE

JOHN A. SHALHOUB

ACHIEVE YOUR GOALS WITH PRIDE

August 2004

A. Achieve your assignments with diligence.

B. Beauty comes from within.

C. Care for your family when they need you.

D. Do always your best, and you will be one of the best.

E. Everyone should work to eat.

F. Friends are good to have if they are honest and loyal.

G. Get a good education and have a good career.

H. Honesty is your best treasure.

I. Initiate charitable actions and receive support.

J. Jealousy can ruin your life.

K. Kindness is the first action toward having good friends.

L. Love and forgiveness can heal all wounds.

PROVERBS ARE THE JOURNEY OF LIFE

M. Manners matter, and so do you.

N. "No" means no, and "yes" means yes.

O. Outstanding performance oftentimes receives praise.

P. Please others with good manners.

Q. Accept others the way they are.

R. Respect grown-ups and be a humble person.

S. Shine with your good grades and good behavior.

T. Treat others the way you want to be treated.

U. Use your time wisely and your mind efficiently.

V. Volunteer your time and you are appreciated.

W. Work with those who appreciate your work.

X. X-out laziness and check-in persistence.

Y. You need to take care of yourself.

Z. Zero adds value if you place it to the right.

JOHN A. SHALHOUB

A GOOD CITIZEN MEETS HIS OBLIGATIONS

A GOOD CITIZEN MEETS HIS OBLIGATIONS

PROVERBS ARE THE JOURNEY OF LIFE

A GOOD CITIZEN MEETS HIS OBLIGATIONS

28 August 2003

A. A Good citizen fulfills their obligations without delay.

B. Be the best you can be in education and good manners.

C. Correct your mistakes and learn valuable lessons from them.

D. Always do your best in whatever you undertake.

E. Earn good grades and take pride in your achievements.

F. Fighting should never be anyone's goal.

G. Good grades are sweet; they bloom like flowers.

H. Health and healing are among life's greatest gifts.

I. Incense smells delightful, just like good manners.

J. Jail is for those who repeatedly harm others.

K. Keep up the good work and stay consistent.

L. Learn all you can and climb the ladder of success.

M. Make good grades to secure a quality education.

N. An "N" grade means there's room for improvement.

O. Outstanding performance always attracts admiration.

P. Prayer heals the broken heart and soothes the unhappy soul.

Q. Quiet down; don't disrupt the class.

R. Responsibility carries more value when paired with accountability.

S. Sitting idle and doing nothing is a sign of laziness.

T. Telling the truth reflects honesty and integrity.

U. United we stand; divided we fall.

V. Visualize your future with focus and clarity.

W. Wars rarely serve a constructive purpose.

X. X-Mark off completed tasks to signify they're done.

Y. Take care of yourself; self-care is essential.

Z. Zero is the starting point, but it leads to nothing without effort.

JOHN A. SHALHOUB

AMEND YOUR WAYS WITH GOOD BEHAVIOR

AMEND YOUR WAYS WITH GOOD BEHAVIOR

PROVERBS ARE THE JOURNEY OF LIFE

AMEND YOUR WAYS WITH GOOD BEHAVIOR

28 August 2003

A. Amend your crooked ways and strive to do the right thing.

B. Be a peacemaker, always promoting harmony.

C. Conserve your energy and use it wisely.

D. Do your homework as soon as you get home.

E. Earn good grades and let that be your reward.

F. Follow instructions carefully and pay close attention.

G. Give respect to adults and heed their advice.

H. Have an inquisitive mind, and you will discover answers.

I. Inside your heart, you will find the truth.

J. Judge your work by the results you achieve.

K. Keep your thoughts in check and focus on positivity.

L. Listen to your teachers and understand their guidance.

M. Meet your obligations without hesitation or delay.

N. Neglect your studies, and failure will follow.

O. Outstanding performance is its own prize.

P. Pass your tests with honor and pride.

Q. Quit being disruptive in class and respect the learning space.

R. Resist evil and embrace righteousness.

S. Share your skills with friends and take pride in your growth.

T. Treat others as you wish to be treated.

U. Use kind words and enjoy hearing the same in return.

V. View your future with clarity and optimism.

W. Will you join me in working together for success?

X. X-Ray your mind and choose good thoughts.

Y. You should always listen to the voice of your conscience.

Z. Zero trouble in school equals a good report.

JOHN A. SHALHOUB

ACTIVATE YOUR FAITH WITH HONESTY!

ACTIVATE YOUR FAITH WITH HONESTY!

PROVERBS ARE THE JOURNEY OF LIFE

ACTIVATE YOUR FAITH WITH HONESTY!

28 August 2002

A. Active faith clears your doubts and heals your wounds.

B. Believe in your conscience when it speaks to you.

C. Cooperation makes new things possible.

D. Don't act like a clown; remember, a clown remains a clown.

E. Earn good grades, and your family will be proud.

F. Finish your work efficiently and with professionalism.

G. Good grades bring recognition and praise.

H. Hurt no one and mistreat no one.

I. Insult no one and avoid causing harm.

J. Jobs go first to those with the right education.

K. Keep up the good work, and you will earn your reward.

L. Learning improves both attitude and performance.

M. Master your skills with confidence and pride.

N. No evil act goes unpunished.

O. Obey the truth, and take pride in yourself.

P. Pray that you may recognize the truth.

Q. Quell violence with love and compassion.

R. Race should never determine friendships.

S. Sharing promotes goodwill among people.

T. Think before you speak or act.

U. United we stand; divided we fall.

V. Violence should never be accepted or tolerated.

W. We should strive for love and peace in this world.

X. Xmas celebrates the birth of Christ.

Y. You are an important person.

Z. Zero grades reflect poorly on your report card.

JOHN A. SHALHOUB

ALWAYS SMILE AND BE HAPPY!

ALWAYS SMILE AND BE HAPPY!

PROVERBS ARE THE JOURNEY OF LIFE

ALWAYS SMILE AND BE HAPPY!

29 August 2005

A. Always smile, and the world will smile with you.

B. Be grateful and appreciative of your blessings.

C. Correct your mistakes and learn from them.

D. Do you know what you are doing? (Consider rephrasing for clarity: "Be sure you know what you're doing.")

E. Earn respect by giving respect.

F. Feel proud whenever you do well.

G. Get good grades, and you will receive praise.

H. Have your work done on time.

I. Intelligence requires hard work to fulfill its purpose.

J. Jealousy is as ugly as anger.

K. Kindness helps improve your relationships with others.

L. Lying hurts both you and those involved.

M. Make good grades, and you'll go to college.

N. No more being rude to others. (Consider rephrasing: "Stop being rude to others.")

O. Obey your conscience and always tell the truth.

P. Please say "please" when asking for something.

Q. Quizzes can show your readiness and preparation.

R. Respect your classmates, and they will respect you.

S. Study, and you'll achieve good grades.

T. Treat kids kindly, and they will treat you kindly.

U. Use good manners, and you'll be treated with courtesy.

V. Volunteer your time to help others.
W. Wait your turn patiently.

PROVERBS ARE THE JOURNEY OF LIFE

X. X-out hatred from your heart.

Y. You are special in your own way.

Z. Zip your lips to avoid trouble.

JOHN A. SHALHOUB

ASK YOUR QUESTION AND WAIT FOR AN ANSWER

ASK YOUR QUESTION AND WAIT FOR AN ANSWER

PROVERBS ARE THE JOURNEY OF LIFE

ASK YOUR QUESTION AND WAIT FOR ANSWER

3 September 2024

A. Ask your teacher for help whenever you have a question.

B. Break no dishes and mend relationships whenever possible.

C. Clean your hands before and after eating.

D. Don't talk when the teacher is speaking.

E. Earn a good education to secure a better future.

F. Force no one to accept your views; respect differences.

G. Guns have no place in schools.

H. Help your mother with household chores.

I. Injustice can lead to anger and hostility—always seek fairness.

J. Jail is for those who harm others repeatedly.

K. Keep away from matches, guns, and other dangerous objects.

L. Listen carefully, understand fully, and learn eagerly.

M. Make good friends and treat others with kindness.

N. Never play with knives or other sharp objects.

O. Optimism inspires you to strive for better things in life.

P. Pick up your toys from the floor and make your bed.

Q. Quiet down, listen attentively, and focus.

R. Remove your clothes from the floor and keep your space tidy.

S. Safety comes first when riding your bicycle—wear a helmet!

T. Teachers appreciate it when you listen to them.

U. Unhappy people may act grouchy—be kind and patient.

V. Visit your grandparents and treat them with respect.

W. Wash your hands thoroughly before and after meals.

X. X-out bad behaviors like hitting and learning to be kind.

Y. You should avoid mimicking others rudely.

Z. Zip your lips when it's time to listen and keep your hands to yourself.

JOHN A. SHALHOUB

ASK AND YOU SHALL RECEIVE AN ANSWER

ASK AND YOU SHALL RECEIVE AN ANSWER

PROVERBS ARE THE JOURNEY OF LIFE

ASK AND YOU SHALL RECEIVE AN ANSWER

29 August 2005

A. Ask, and you shall receive what you seek.

B. Be beautiful—inside and out.

C. Care for those in need.

D. Develop your talents wisely.

E. Educate yourself with wisdom.

F. Follow the truth wherever it leads.

G. God gave you a mind; use it well.

H. Honesty means telling the truth.

I. Inclusion makes everyone feel they belong.

J. Jealousy hurts those it touches.

K. Know yourself—who you are and what you want.

L. Liberty grows through education.

M. Maintain composure; don't fall apart.

N. Say no to drugs—always.

- **O.** Obey your conscience and respect your elders.
- **P.** Pick up after yourself and keep your space clean.
- **Q.** Quit pestering others—it's not kind.
- **R.** Respect everyone, even strangers.
- **S.** Silence can save you from trouble.
- **T.** Think before you act.
- **U.** Understand your needs and work to meet them.
- **V.** Victory tastes sweet when you've earned it.
- **W.** Where's your common sense? Use it wisely.
- **X.** X-out bad behavior; embrace the good.
- **Y.** You are what you choose to be.
- **Z.** Zero effort earns zero results—aim higher.

PROVERBS ARE THE JOURNEY OF LIFE

ANSWER WHEN ASKED AND BE RESPECTFUL

ANSWER WHEN ASKED AND BE RESPECTFUL

JOHN A. SHALHOUB

ANSWER WHEN ASKED AND BE RESPECTFUL

9 June 2004

A. Answer when asked and speak when needed.

B. Bees work to make honey; you need to work to make your money.

C. Cooperation is the key to teamwork and success.

D. Do your best in school as well as at home.

E. Enduring your hardships will make you a better person.

F. Flee from evil and be a peacemaker.

G. Give your best effort every day.

H. Healthy body is in a healthy diet.

I. Ignore your violent temper and welcome peace.

J. Just do what is right and walk away from what is wrong.

K. Know that you can make a difference in your life.

L.   Love yourself and you will love others.

M.   Manage your life with care and intelligence.

N.   Navigate your world with diligence.

O.   Obey the truth and you will live in peace.

P.   Peace should be the hope of every loving human being.

Q.   Quell your anger with love and forgiveness.

R.   Remember that what goes up will come down.

S.   Stop your evil ways and listen to the voice of your conscience.

T.   Train your mind to do the right thing.

U.   Understand that doing the right thing is a good thing. V.   Reflect on your thoughts and keep up with your responsibilities.

W.   Watch your steps; see where you're going.

X. X is an X, but faith is hope for a better life.

Y. You must love yourself for who you really are.

Z. Z is twisted, but your mind shouldn't be clear.

ALLOW YOURSELF TO GROW WITH DIGNITY!

ALLOW YOURSELF TO GROW WITH DIGNITY!

JOHN A. SHALHOUB

ALLOW YOURSELF TO GROW WITH DIGNITY!

30 August 2024

A. Allow yourself to grow and glow.
B. Be kind to other kids when you play with them.
C. Care for the feelings of others.
D. Discipline will help you to be organized and focused.
E. Education is important for you and me.
F. Feel safe and you will be safe.
G. Give others respect and you will receive respect.
H. Help people when they're hurt.
I. I use my hands to help and not hurt.
J. Jail is for those who purposely hurt people.
K. Keep guns out of the reach of the children.
L. Lying will cause harm and pain to family and friends.

PROVERBS ARE THE JOURNEY OF LIFE

M. Manners are important. Say please and thank you.

N. No hitting, pushing, or shoving are allowed in school.

O. Oppose violence and seek peace.

P. Pick up your trash, don't litter.

Q. Quit smoking; eat healthy food.

R. Respect the people who care for you.

S. Sound mind is in a sound body.

T. Treat others the way you want to be treated.

U. U-turn may take you away from the main road.

V. Violence will cause people to hurt one another.

W. Wise words can save one's life.

X. X-disrespect out and check good manners in.

Y. You should not annoy anyone.

Z. Zip your mouth and listen when others talk.

JOHN A. SHALHOUB

TREAT ALL PEOPLE FAIRLY

TREAT ALL PEOPLE FAIRLY

PROVERBS ARE THE JOURNEY OF LIFE

TREAT ALL PEOPLE FAIRLY

30 August 2024

A. All people should be treated fairly.

B. Better things await those who love the Lord.

C. Courage gives you the energy to do daring things.

D. Drugs are dangerous and harmful to your health.

E. Education helps you learn and grow.

F. Forgive others, even when they don't apologize.

G. Greet people with courtesy and respect.

H. Help others in their time of need.

I. It's important to complete your tasks promptly.

J. Judge people fairly and kindly.

K. Keep your hands and feet to yourself.

L. Listen, even when you don't like the person.

M. Make good friends and treat them well.

N. No one is perfect except God.

O. Open schools and strive to reduce crime.

P. Patience is the road to peace.

Q. A quick temper is like gunpowder—both can cause harm.

R. Respect the rights and dignity of others.

S. Smoking is hazardous to your health.

T. Treat others the way you want to be treated.

U. Unity creates strength, while disunity leads to weakness.

V. Vegetables are essential for a healthy diet.

W. We are responsible for our actions.

X. X-ray your thoughts and address your flaws.

Y. You need to practice self-control.

Z. Zip your lips when it's better to stay silent.

PROVERBS ARE THE JOURNEY OF LIFE

ALWAYS HAVE A POSITIVE ATTITUDE

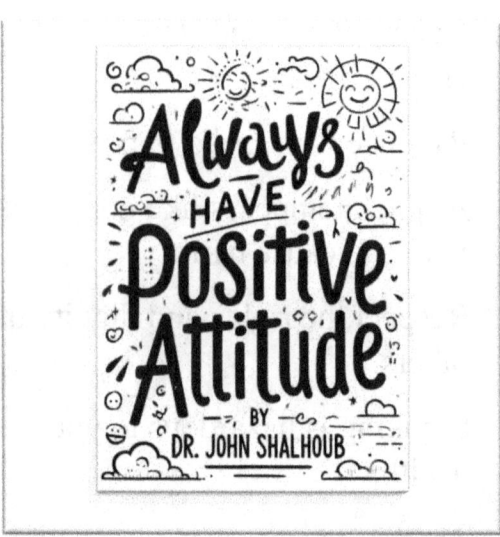

ALWAYS HAVE A POSITIVE ATTITUDE

JOHN A. SHALHOUB

ALWAYS HAVE A POSITIVE ATTITUDE

31 August 2003

A. Always maintain a positive attitude.

B. Be kind and friendly to your friends.

C. Call people by their names—it shows respect.

D. Don't be rude or lose your temper.

E. Earn good grades, and you'll feel proud of yourself.

F. Follow directions carefully instead of guessing.

G. Give food to someone in need, and you'll be blessed.

H. Hitting someone will only get you into trouble.

I. Integrity is like jasmine—it has a fragrance that's admired by all.

J. Join friends who are hardworking and do well in school.

K. Keep up with your homework to stay on track.

- **L.** Laughing without reason can sometimes seem disrespectful.
- **M.** Master a skill, and you'll never go hungry.
- **N.** Nice people tend to attract nice friends.
- **O.** Open the door for your mother or anyone in need—it's courteous.
- **P.** Pay attention to your teacher and follow instructions.
- **Q.** Quit bothering others—it's unkind and disruptive.
- **R.** Responsibility and respect build strong character.
- **S.** Stand up when a guest enters your home to show respect.
- **T.** Talking back to a teacher is disrespectful and inappropriate.
- **U.** Understand the rules and respect authorities.
- **V.** Volunteer your time to help others—it's rewarding.

W. When you make a mistake, face it—don't run away.

X. Xmas is a joyful time to cherish with family.

Y. You should listen to and obey your parents—they care about you.

Z. Zip your lips when staying silent is the best option.

PROVERBS ARE THE JOURNEY OF LIFE

ACCEPT ME AS I AM!

ACCEPT ME AS I AM!

JOHN A. SHALHOUB

ACCEPT ME AS I AM!

1 September 2002

A. Accept yourself as you are, and you'll feel better.

B. Brush your teeth and wash your face daily.

C. Clean your hands before and after meals.

D. Do what your mom asks you to do.

E. Embrace an easy-going attitude in all you do.

F. Follow the rules and respect your parents.

G. Give your full attention to teachers and parents.

H. Help others when they need it.

I. Inquire about details before making decisions.

J. Jealousy is worse than a disease—it can destroy you.

PROVERBS ARE THE JOURNEY OF LIFE

K. Kindness to your siblings brings joy to everyone.

L. Listen attentively when someone is speaking.

M. Make progress by dedicating time to your books.

N. Never use offensive language.

O. Obey your parents and teachers without hesitation.

P. Pay close attention to instructions.

Q. Quick thinking can save you in critical moments.

R. Respect the truth, and you'll sleep peacefully.

S. Speak kind words to others.

T. Thank those who teach you good values and manners.

U. Understand the truth and always stand by it.

V. Value life and cherish its beauty.

W. Waste no time; time is precious.

X. X-out sloppy performance and poor work.

Y. Yield to your teacher's authority without talking back.

Z. Zero effort equals zero results—strive for success.

PROVERBS ARE THE JOURNEY OF LIFE

ALWAYS BE POLITE TO OTHERS

ALWAYS BE POLITE TO OTHERS

JOHN A. SHALHOUB

ALWAYS BE POLITE TO OTHERS

3 September 2024

A. Always be polite and courteous.

B. Build schools, and you will close jails.

C. Cling to the truth, and it will save you.

D. Don't use hurtful words; they can create deep scars.

E. Earn good grades and be proud of yourself.

F. Finish your work and follow directions.

G. Give your teacher your undivided attention.

H. Happy kids treat each other with kindness.

I. If you don't listen, you don't learn.

J. Join your friends, enjoy time together, and avoid fights.

K. Keep your hands and feet to yourself.

L. Listen to your teacher and follow their instructions.

M. Manners matter, as does your family.

PROVERBS ARE THE JOURNEY OF LIFE

N. Name your tune, sing your song, and be happy.

O. Obedience builds your parents' trust.

P. Pay attention and follow directions carefully.

Q. Quiet down in class while the teacher is teaching.

R. Respect your parents, teachers, and classmates.

S. Stop talking when the teacher is speaking.

T. Take a time-out to reflect on mistakes.

U. A negative attitude reflects poorly on you.

V. Visit your grandparents and make them smile.

W. Water your plants and watch them grow.

X. X-out bad influences from your life.

Y. Year by year, guide your life in a positive direction.

Z. Zip your lips and open your ears.

JOHN A. SHALHOUB

CHAPTER SEVEN
PROVERBS ARE THE WAY OF

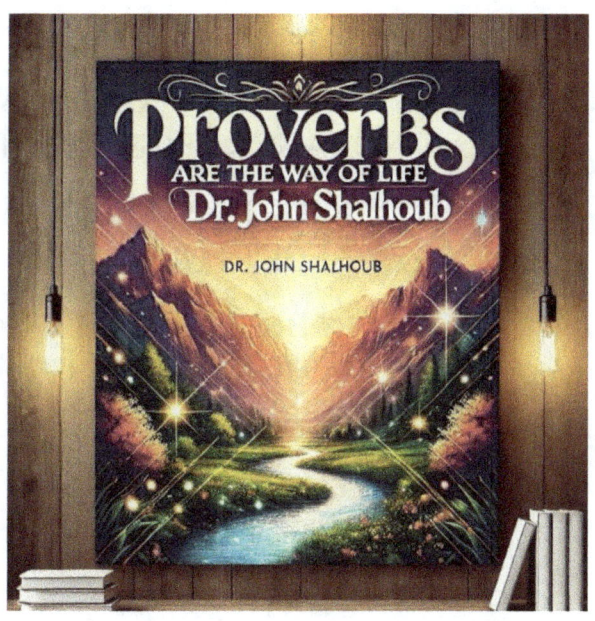

LIFE

PROVERBS ARE THE WAY OF LIFE

PROVERBS ARE THE WAY OF LIFE

Inspirational, Motivational, Vocational Proverbs

Educational Proverbs:

- IGNORANCE BEGETS IGNORANCE, AND IGNORANCE BEGETS MISERY.
- POVERTY BEGETS POVERTY, AND POVERTY BEGETS HUNGER.
- EDUCATION BEGETS EDUCATION, AND EDUCATION BEGETS GOOD JOBS.
- A GOOD ATTITUDE IS THE FOUNDATION OF SUCCESS!

JOHN A. SHALHOUB

GOOD EDUCATION PROVERBS ARE THE MAP FOR A BETTER LIFE!

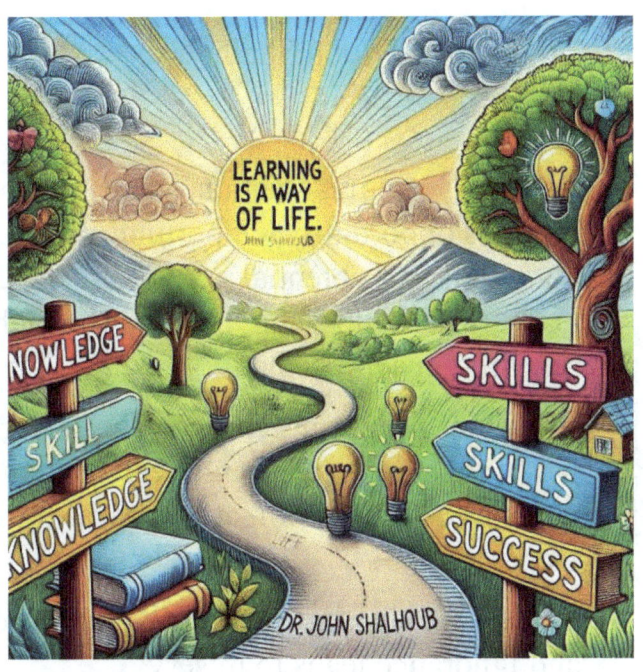

GOOD EDUCATION PROVERBS ARE THE MAP FOR A BETTER LIFE!

GOOD EDUCATION PROVERBS ARE THE MAP FOR A BETTER LIFE!

By

Dr. Fr. John Shalhoub

15 May 2000

1. Success requires action, and action requires opportunity. Opportunity creates potential, and potential sets goals. Goals lead to activities and plans, ultimately resulting in achievement.

2. Trustworthiness, integrity, and hard work will enrich your mind and heart, helping you succeed in school, at home, or in the workplace.

3. Remember, ignorance breeds ignorance, and ignorance leads to misery.

4. Poverty leads to more poverty, and poverty leads to hunger.

    Lazy people do not climb the ladder to better jobs.

5. Education leads to more education, which opens doors to good jobs, honor, and dignity.

6. Plan, and you will get ahead. A new world will open before you.

7. The future is in your hands. Cultivate your life like you would till the land, and you will reap a fruitful harvest.

8. Good teaching involves creativity, innovation, and determination to make a difference in students' lives.

9. Good character is the glue that binds your life to happiness, fulfillment, and contentment.

10. Good character is the foundation of honesty, integrity, and success.

11. Good character leads to respect, honor, and better relations.

12. Learning is about gaining applicable knowledge and applying it in a constructive way.

13. Good character is the key to a better life. Traits like honesty, integrity, responsibility, cooperation, fairness, loyalty, citizenship, and trustworthiness should guide your life.

14. You are the fruit of life—be the seed of a better life every day.

15. Education is the willingness to gain knowledge and apply it positively.

16. Hope, ambition, courage, respect, caring, and sharing lead to a happy society.

17. Good character is the foundation for a better life, and education sets you free.
18. Faith is the engine of the heart, and the heart is the source of kindness and love.
19. Boredom, laziness, and loneliness erode the spirit, disturb peace, and breed unhappiness.
20. Wherever your job is, there your loyalty should be. Be faithful and loyal to your job, and don't cut corners.
21. If you don't read, you won't eat. Open your books and study every day.
22. Children reflect on their families and society. Raise them well to be the future's strength.
23. A broom without bristles isn't a broom, and a leader without followers isn't a leader.
24. Those who challenge the wind will face the storm, and those who seek trouble will find it.
25. The secret of victory isn't in how high you rise but in how humble you remain.
26. If life fails you, don't fail yourself. Keep trying as long as you have the energy and will to work toward success.

27. Life is God's ultimate gift. Do not abuse it; live with honor and dignity.

28. Ignorance stems from laziness, and success comes from motivation.

29. A smile a day keeps stress at bay. Make your life more peaceful and joyful.

30. If you punish a student without offering a positive alternative, you will do them a disservice.

31. The family that prays and eats together stays together.

32. Always take time to play, share, and have fun with your children.

33. Listen to your children, engage in conversation with them, and be open to their ideas.

34. Be loving, tolerant, and patient with your children—they are the future.

35. Don't be a poor role model for your children; they need your love, not just your orders.

36. Never scold or spank your children in public. You want their respect, not their fear.

37. Help your children make their own decisions and solve their own problems.

PROVERBS ARE THE JOURNEY OF LIFE

38. Be present when your children need your help and attention.

39. Children are your future treasures and support. Be there for them always.

40. Money doesn't grow on trees, but fruit does. The more trees you plant, the more fruit you will have.

41. Life and schools teach wisdom, faith, patience, and skills, but we must be open to learning.

42. Children don't need to live in castles; they need loving, caring parents.

43. Misery knows no color, and prejudice has no face. Let us be brothers and sisters to each other.

44. Ignorance, laziness, and prejudice are enemies of both the mind and society.

45. Poverty will follow if you lead the way. Education opens doors to good jobs.

46. Life is a jungle—if you forget your path, you'll get lost and devoured.

47. Everything in life has a place, every word has a meaning, and you are equally important.

48. When loneliness speaks to you, it's time to speak with someone you trust.

49. Please don't raise your voice. I can hear you—just speak calmly and respectfully.

50. Listen to me, and I will understand you. Don't fight with me; be kind and open-minded.

51. Be a good role model for your children so they can learn from you.

52. Children are creative. Let them make decisions and take risks.

53. Explain the world's dangers to your children, but be there to protect them.

54. Teach your children to stand ready and prepared to combat evil with courage, perseverance, and skill.

55. Allow your children to take responsibility for their actions.

56. Supervise your children to ensure they oversee their own activities.

57. Never ridicule your children or insult their intelligence.

    Instead, encourage them.

58. Provide your children with realistic expectations, working within the bounds of their abilities.

59. Let your children act their age. Don't smother their choices and freedom.

60. Praise your children and encourage them, even when you disagree with them.

61. Do not burden your children with guilt when things don't go well or when they feel frustrated with their work.

62. Help your children overcome their frustration by empathizing with them and showing them the right way to approach things.

63. Allow your children to ask questions. Answer them truthfully.

64. Do not expect your children to be perfect, but don't expect them to fail, either.

65. Help your children understand both their strengths and weaknesses.

66. Be a good role model for your children. Let your relationship be gentle, kind, and comforting, free from domination, disruption, or intimidation.

67. Be understanding, compassionate, and loving, especially when your children are in the wrong.

68. Give your children the time and space to respect and get to know you.

69. Hug your children and express kindness and love openly.

70. Encourage your children, even when they make mistakes or fail in their tasks.
71. Be present and proactive when your children need you.
72. Always know where your children are.
73. Let your children know where you are as well.
74. He who bites the dust will be buried in it. Laziness leads to poverty.
75. The one who wins a fight is the one who avoids getting into one.
76. When in conflict with another person, try to resolve it by talking it over with them.
77. When things don't go your way, learn to absorb the blows like a sponge or sway like a reed in the wind.
78. While mankind has made technological and scientific advances, it still lacks moral and spiritual growth.
79. Motivation without a plan or focus is like a wheel that doesn't spin.
80. No matter how rich you are, you must pay the price for your actions, just like everyone else.
81. What matters most is being in control of your own life.

82. A person who doesn't respect those who are kind and honest lacks integrity and trustworthiness.

83. Those who are unhappy at work without pay will still be unhappy, even with pay.

84. The person who steals an egg will steal a horse.

85. The one who doesn't give up is the one who will win in the end.

86. The person who reaches the depths of their soul is the one who converses with God.

87. The person who treats you as they treat themselves is fair.

88. Education without inspiration is like religion without prayer.

89. A society that doesn't provide its members with education, healthcare, and job opportunities is destined for failure and disintegration.

90. Passion is like makeup; it wears off quickly. Be genuine and candid in your relationships.

91. A rich man thinks of money, but a hungry man thinks of a loaf of bread.

92. Love is like gold; the more you polish it, the more it shines.

93. A nation that lacks inspiration for education will slide into mediocrity and disintegration.

94. Bigotry is like corrosion; it destroys itself and everything it touches.

95. The secret to success in education is listening to your teachers and doing the work.

96. Ugliness, like laziness, isolates you the more you have of it.

97. Smile at the world, and the world will smile back.

98. Misery has no color, and a loaf of bread has no loyalty.

99. Observe the stars, look beyond the horizon, and be free.

100. A nation that destroys its own talented and skilled people is doomed to fail.

101. Parents, always know where your children are.

102. Students, always know where your books are.

103. Teachers, always know where your students are in your classroom.

104. Politicians, always know where your constituents are in your district.

105. Don't buy a coat and then examine its quality. Examine it before you buy it.

106. If the heat in the kitchen is too high, turn down the thermostat.

107. Education sets you free, while ignorance traps you in your own chains.

108. Time is as precious as the air you breathe and the water you drink. Use it wisely, and you will triumph.

109. Education gives you vision, while ignorance leaves you blind.

110. Seek peace, and you will live in peace. Seek war, and you will die in war.

111. Hard work conquers everything, while laziness helps you accomplish nothing.

112. Deception, pride, and vanity are self-destructive. Be honest and truthful.

113. Stay positive, and you will feel good all over!

114. Grow like a weed, work like honeybees, and blossom like flowers.

115. Children, education is your path to success. You are the future of the world.

116. Children do not abuse your lives. With education, you will master your own destiny.

117. Children, I cannot do for you that you can do for yourselves.

118. The fruits of victory are sweet when you love what you do and do what you love.

119. Peace will triumph when prejudice and violence among nations come to an end.

120. Education gives you the key to two doors: one to success and one to defeat. The choice is yours.

121. Changes include removing redundancies, improving sentence clarity, and fixing minor grammatical issues. The flow is also slightly adjusted for better readability.'

122. Your passage is well-written, but there are a few areas where grammar, punctuation, and flow can be improved for

    better clarity and impact. Here's a revised version with those adjustments:

123. Education for the mind is like food for the body.

124. Don't be disrespectful to anyone; if you are, you'll only disrespect yourself.

125. Ignorance and laziness are the breeding grounds for troublemakers and beggars.

126. Education and learning skills are the playground for the mind. Play the game well, or don't count yourself in.

127. If you make a fool of yourself, what do you expect from others?

128. Education and learning are the door to success; open it, and you'll find a treasure awaiting you.

129. Fairness, consistency, and persistence are the best tools for disciplining children.

130. You must educate and discipline your children to take responsibility for their actions.

131. It's better to build schools for children than to build jails for adults.

132. Sound decisions usually favor the prepared and skilled mind.

133. We must work hard, be productive, and enjoy the fruits of our labor!

134. Profanity is an evil curse, while a sweet tongue is gentler than a breeze.

135. Hard work, confidence, guidance, trust, learning, achievement, and patience are

the products of good character and discipline.

136. God builds the brain, we build the school, and together, we run the world's affairs.

137. Punishment without good alternatives bears no good fruit.

138. Don't ask me, "How do you feel?" unless you're willing to listen.

139. The secret of success in life is not to do what you like but to like what you do.

140. The mind will excel once books become your friends and playground.

141. Alcohol, drugs, and gambling are the enemies of humanity.

142. Education is your lifejacket in this troubled world.

143. Let us tell the truth and be free, for telling lies makes us slaves to evil minds.

144. Laziness begets boredom, and boredom begets poverty!

145. Don't get tired of learning new things! Learn from the honeybee that makes honey.

146. Great success is achieved when students meet their books, not when they run the streets.

147. It's not your aptitude, but your attitude, that determines your altitude.

148. If you do not seek education, poverty will seek you.

149. The price for foolishness today is a reprimand, but tomorrow, it may be your life.

150. Don't waste time questioning rules and regulations. Focus on learning new information to graduate and move forward in life.

151. It's better to build "in-school suspension" programs for irresponsible students than to build jails for irresponsible adults.

152. Education is the key to good careers and jobs in life.

153. Teachers are the hinges that swing open the doors of knowledge, discipline, and learning for students.

154. If you don't use your mind, it will get rusty. Learn a skill, and you'll never go hungry.

155. Don't tire of learning new skills; they'll help you achieve better things in life.

156. Laziness is like a rock that sinks to the bottom, while success is like a diamond that sparkles on your finger.

157. Hard work and perseverance conquer everything in life and bring you to the doorstep of glory.

158. A motivated student doesn't wait for the work to come to him; he goes after it.

159. Silence is sacred because it carries you beyond yourself.

160. School is the mosaic house of inspiration, development, vision, and maturity.

161. School is not a house of comfort but a place of learning and planning for the future.

162. A student without a pen is like a soldier without a gun.

163. Don't be a fallen angel behind closed doors.

164. Daydreaming in class won't help you pass.

165. A friend in need is like gold hidden deep.

166. Let your fingers walk to your books, and your ears listen to your teacher.

167. If a teacher asks you to do your assignment, don't argue— just do it.

168. School is a building with classrooms filled with tomorrow's future.

PROVERBS ARE THE JOURNEY OF LIFE

169. If you don't do your teacher's assigned work, don't expect more than a big "F."
170. Silence, listening, and studying will help you learn.
171. Knowledge without manners is like a bird without feathers.
172. The ambitious mind will bloom like a flower!
173. If you don't learn from your mistakes, you'll fall flat on your face.
174. He who dances his life away will end up living a beggar's

    life.
175. Silence is a way to know yourself and reach beyond your soul.
176. Responsibility, learning, and hard work are the keys to success.
177. Children are the future of humanity; teach them well.
178. Tell me who you associate with, and I will tell you who you are.
179. Going to school late is like arriving late to your own wedding—you may never know if the bride is still waiting.

180. Be free like a bird and spread good things throughout your life.

181. When misery knocks, don't open the door.

182. Always tell the truth, and you'll live as a free person.

183. A real loser is someone who surrenders control of his life to defeatism.

184. Wanted: Students and textbooks to teach. No references are required.

185. Our most valuable riches in life—like love and kindness—are free.

186. Drinking and driving are dangerous. Be smart and know your limit.

187. Falling asleep in class won't help you pass.

188. Learn a skill now, or you'll regret it later.

189. Help! I was caught in my own trap, doing the wrong thing.

190. Yours is not to question why the teacher teaches this or that; yours is to study and pass.

191. The family is an institution of life on Earth. Honor your family, respect your

teachers, know your friends, and be true to yourself.

192. Stop, think, listen, learn, and grow up, and your life will be happier.

193. Learn to spell, and you'll do well. This skill will help you get a good job.

194. If you don't obey, you will pay! There's a consequence for every action.

195. Develop sound thinking and watch how well you'll bloom.

196. Drugs won't help you reach your goals, but good grades will.

197. He who fails to remember the past sips from the cup of doom.

198. Say yes to school, education, and learning—and say no to drugs, alcohol, and smoking.

199. Education can take you a long way toward self-fulfillment.

200. A man who refuses to face his problems is like an ostrich burying its head in the sand.

201. Grades aren't given; they're earned. You must study to graduate.

202. Your body is shaped by what you eat, but your mind is shaped by what you learn.

203. Dress well, look nice, and be proud of yourself.

204. Your child will say, "Teach me; don't threaten me." Don't assume I have all the answers.

205. See how hard the bad ones fall! Why would you follow their ways?

206. Good grades are like a bouquet of flowers—they look good and smell good.

207. You're gambling with your life when you drink and drive.

208. Trust yourself when others doubt you. Keep up the good work.

209. A student with bad grades is like someone carrying a bouquet of dead flowers.

210. No pain, no gain, and no learning. Don't expect to graduate without working for it.

211. Once in pain, you feel the pain, but once in jail, there's no gain.

212. When justice leads to injustice, the well-being of humanity is in jeopardy.

213. Always thank the one who teaches you a new skill, not the one who just wants to play and have fun.

214. Education provides a way out of poverty; ignorance leads straight to poverty and misery.

215. When the storm strikes and fear takes over, faith and hope will come to the rescue.

216. My friend, if I can't help you learn a skill, I'm not a good teacher.

217. Unless the heart is honest and sincere, all the courts and laws in the world won't bring integrity and peace to the land.

218. My friend, if I know you, I know myself. If I don't know myself, I don't know you.

219. If I mistreat others without cause, I will be drinking from the cup of damnation.

220. Don't talk to me while you're looking up, nor look down. Let's sit or stand together; we are both equals.

JOHN A. SHALHOUB

CHAPTER EIGHT
THE VARIOUS THEMES ON BEHAVIOR AND GOOD

EDUCATION

EDUCATION AND GOOD BEHAVIOR FOR A CIVIL AND PEACEFUL SOCIETY

PROVERBS ARE THE JOURNEY OF LIFE

EDUCATION AND GOOD BEHAVIOR FOR A CIVIL AND PEACEFUL SOCIETY

EDUCATION AND GOOD BEHAVIOR FOR A CIVIL AND PEACEFUL SOCIETY

JOHN A. SHALHOUB

I BELIEVE IN EDUCATION, HARD WORK AND ACHIEVEMENT

I BELIEVE IN EDUCATION, HARD WORK AND ACHIEVEMENT

PROVERBS ARE THE JOURNEY OF LIFE

I BELIEVE IN EDUCATION, HARD WORK AND ACHIEVEMENT

9 November 2024

- I believe in Character Education as my moral guide. It will enlighten me and make my life more meaningful.
- I believe in treating others with respect, honesty, and integrity.
- I value self-discipline, organization, and time management.
- I believe in showing initiative, fostering cooperation, and practicing patience to do my best.
- I embrace caring, sharing, and helping one another.
- I believe I can change and grow to become a better person.
- I strive to be firm, self-motivated, and determined to achieve my goals.

- I value manners, courtesies, and compassion.
- I recognize the importance of apologizing, forgiving, and making amends.
- I believe in working together to create a better world—one that is safe and secure, free from violence and oppression.
- I believe in my ability to be trustworthy and a responsible citizen.

PROVERBS ARE THE JOURNEY OF LIFE

CHARACTER AND DISCIPLINE, I WANT!

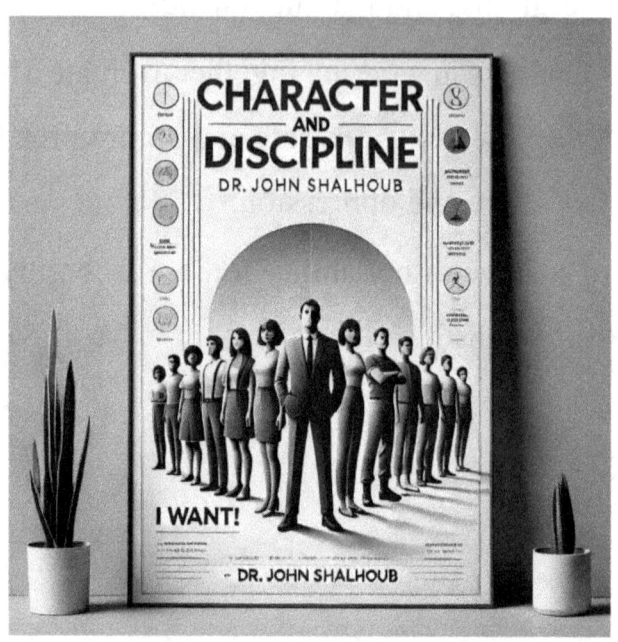

CHARACTER AND DISCIPLINE, I WANT!

JOHN A. SHALHOUB

CHARACTER AND DISCIPLINE, I WANT!

15 August 2009

Character is my trait,
a trait I like to hold and keep.

Character is like a seed in the ground,
It has grown big and made me feel good and proud.

Character teaches me to respect others
and care for everyone.
It enriches me with kindness and respect.

Character teaches me to love others,
And be nice to my family and friends.

Character I like to have and maintain.
It makes me feel good and great.

PROVERBS ARE THE JOURNEY OF LIFE

Character is my motto.
It teaches me honesty and integrity.

Would you like to join me in standing for character
At church, home, and school?

Character is what I want and need.
Character is what we all need and want.

Would you join in with me and sing a song,
Character is for you and me.
Character is for you and me.
Character is what we all need!
Character is what we all need!

JOHN A. SHALHOUB

PLAN AHEAD

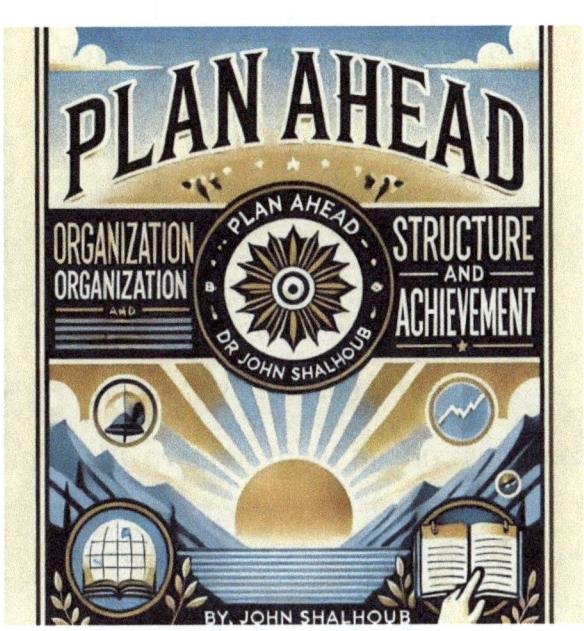

PLAN AHEAD

PROVERBS ARE THE JOURNEY OF LIFE

PLAN AHEAD!

Plan, use your head, and be glad.
Don't be lazy; don't lie in bed.
Don't be sad; just be glad.

Get up; make your bed.
Be ready; get your school bag
and be ready to go to school with Dad.

Be ready for school; don't be mad.
Be glad; listen to your dad.

Think, plan.
Don't tease the cat; don't be bad.
Go with dad!

Go to school with Dad.
Say you're glad and not mad, and you're not bad.

JOHN A. SHALHOUB

Plan; be glad. You're going to school, to learn from Mrs. Pat.

Now, Mom is glad; Dad is glad, and Ms. Pat is glad.

Plan; be glad.
You're not mad, you're not sad, and you're not bad in class.

PROVERBS ARE THE JOURNEY OF LIFE

ENCOURAGE ME

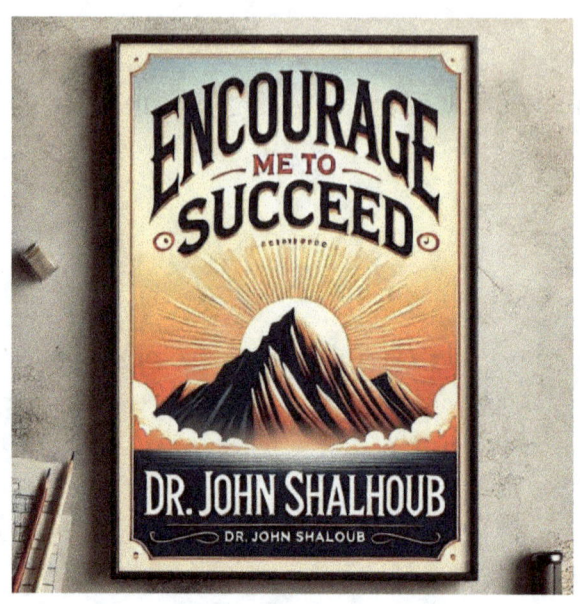

ENCOURAGE ME

JOHN A. SHALHOUB

ENCOURAGE ME

Encourage me to learn, to improve and to be efficient.

Encourage me to be patient, kind, and thoughtful.

Encourage me to be friendly, courteous and peaceful.

Encourage me to listen, understand and follow directions.

Encourage me to be productive, supportive and positive.

Encourage me to be helpful, tolerant and respectful.

PROVERBS ARE THE JOURNEY OF LIFE

Encourage me to be honest, truthful and responsible,

and at the end of the day, I may hear,

"Job well done!"

JOHN A. SHALHOUB

HELP ME SEE THE WAY

HELP ME SEE THE WAY

PROVERBS ARE THE JOURNEY OF LIFE

HELP ME SEE THE WAY

My complaints are:
I don't listen to my teachers, read my textbooks and do my homework.

My regrets are:
I am making no progress, getting low grades, and have no more pride.
So, I won't be graduating!

My fears are:
I don't have a degree, or skills.
I don't have a good job awaiting me when I leave school.
Woe is me!
What is going to become of me?
Help me to see the light.
I want to be somebody!
Yes! Somebody!

JOHN A. SHALHOUB

I want to learn all I can learn.
I can learn, please show me the way.

I want to be on my way to glory.
Help me. Be my friend!
Be my guide! Be my hope!

I have begun to see the light.
Lead the way.

I will follow you to my victory.

PROVERBS ARE THE JOURNEY OF LIFE

I WILL MAKE IT, I WILL GRADUATE!

I WILL MAKE IT, I WILL GRADUATE!

JOHN A. SHALHOUB

I WILL MAKE IT, I GRADUATE!

I will listen to my teacher, read my books,
Do my homework, and ask others to help me.

My goal is to get good grades, learn new skills,
and have a good career.

I am determined to listen, ask questions
and know what I don't know.

I will earn my degree; enjoy my education,
And live an honest and honorable life!

PROVERBS ARE THE JOURNEY OF LIFE

I DRESS RIGHT

I DRESS RIGHT

JOHN A. SHALHOUB

I DRESS RIGHT

I dress right; I look right.
I don't look sloppy or shaggy.
I look nice; I look happy.
I like going to school.

I am clean; I look clean.
I stay neat and clean.

I comb my hair; I wash my face.
I wear neat clothes all day long.

I am bright; I look bright.
I do my schoolwork.
I am kind; I am friendly.
I feel good about myself.

I listen and follow directions.
I study for my quizzes and tests.

I get good grades.

I am a responsible student.

I am always ready and prepared.

I am a proud student.

I am a conscientious person.

I stay out of trouble.

I don't fight with anyone.

I am a good student.

I am a good citizen.

JOHN A. SHALHOUB

RESPECT

RESPECT

RESPECT

I respect you; you respect me.
We need to be kind and friendly.

I care for you; you care for me.
I want you to help me.
I want you to be nice and gentle.

I work with you; you work with me.
And see how happy we can be.

I behave; I listen; I follow directions.
I obey my teacher.
I obey my mom and dad.
I trust you; you trust me.
I am trustworthy; you're trustworthy.
We all have trust and honesty.
We have integrity.
We are all proud citizens.

JOHN A. SHALHOUB

We do our work diligently.

Respect I need so I can be happy.

Respect is needed so that we may Live together in harmony.

PROVERBS ARE THE JOURNEY OF LIFE

I AM IN CONTROL

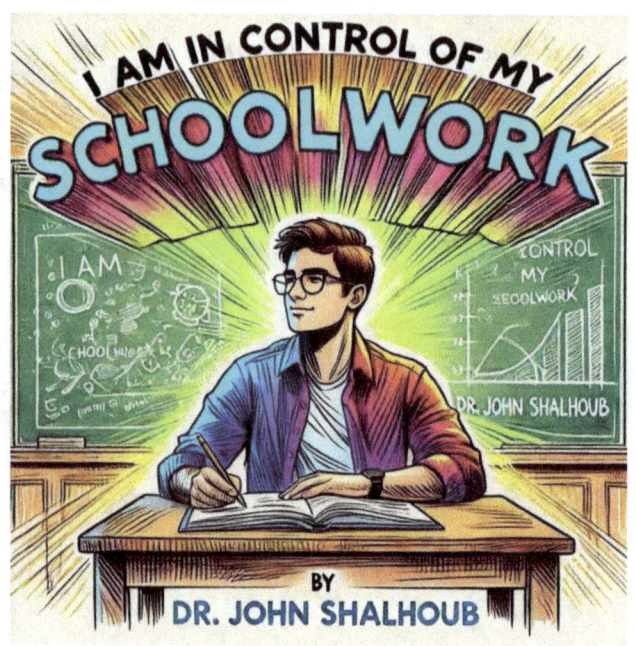

I AM IN CONTROL

JOHN A. SHALHOUB

I AM IN CONTROL

I am in control of my mind,
I am in control of my space.

I listen.
I listen to my mom and dad.
I listen to my teacher; I truly listen.
I listen.

I am in control of my body.
I am in control of my hands and feet.
I behave in class.
I don't talk and disrupt.
I listen.

I listen to my mom and dad.
I listen to my teacher; I truly listen.

I listen.

PROVERBS ARE THE JOURNEY OF LIFE

I am in control of my voice; I am nice.
I speak nicely and softly.
I say nice things; I say please and thank you.

I listen.
I listen to my mom and dad.
I listen to my teacher; I truly listen.

I am in control of my space.
I don't throw stuff on the floor.
I keep my area clean,
I don't roll on the floor.

I listen.
I listen to my mom and dad.
I listen to my teacher; I truly listen.

JOHN A. SHALHOUB

I BELIEVE IN DISCIPLINE

I BELIEVE IN DISCIPLINE

PROVERBS ARE THE JOURNEY OF LIFE

I BELIEVE IN DISCIPLINE IN MY LIFE

*I believe in discipline what I need
for it helps me to be a good person.*

*I believe in caring for my family and friends,
And trusting them to help me when I need them.*

*I believe in setting goals for my life,
And working hard to achieve them.*

*I believe in organizing my time wisely,
And planning my daily work.*

*I believe in time management,
And having a good, positive attitude toward everyone.*

*I believe in high expectations,
And working hard to achieve success.*

JOHN A. SHALHOUB

I believe in ambition, working hard,
And using my time wisely.

I believe you and I can be a good team to learn,
Help and support each other.

I believe that discipline is what I want for you
and me from sunrise to sunset.

I believe in going to bed on time,
Waking up on time and doing my work on time.

I am proud of my work. I am proud of myself.
I am happy to be me.

Discipline is for you and me.

PROVERBS ARE THE JOURNEY OF LIFE

I AM A TRUSTWORTHY PERSON

I AM A TRUSTWORTHY PERSON

JOHN A. SHALHOUB

I AM A TRUSTWORTHY PERSON

I am happy and friendly.

I am trustworthy.

I am reliable, dependable, and accountable.

I am trustworthy.

I am honest, truthful, and forthright.

I am trustworthy.

I am genuine, kind, and friendly.

I am trustworthy.

I am attentive, obedient, and law-abiding.

I am trustworthy.

I am careful, patient and loyal.

I am trustworthy.

PROVERBS ARE THE JOURNEY OF LIFE

I am positive, warm, and helpful.
I am trustworthy.

I don't cuss, lie or cheat.
I am trustworthy.

I don't smoke, drink or do drugs.
I am trustworthy.

I love my family, country and school.
I am trustworthy.

I am diligent, organized, and persistent.
I am trustworthy.
I am a proud citizen.

JOHN A. SHALHOUB

COOPERATION

COOPERATION

COOPERATION

I help you; you help me and see how happy we can be.

I work with you, and you work with me.

We are nice and friendly.

I learn to write, read, and play safely.

I learn manners at home, school, and church.

We say please and thank you.

I listen to my mom and dad.

I follow their directions.

I obey them and say, "Yes sir and yes ma'am."

JOHN A. SHALHOUB

I am a team player.

I do my chores and pay attention when my teacher speaks to me.

I am your friend. You are my friend.
We need each other.

Let us do a job well done.

PROVERBS ARE THE JOURNEY OF LIFE

I AM A RESPONSIBLE PERSON

I AM A RESPONSIBLE PERSON

JOHN A. SHALHOUB

I AM A RESPONSIBLE PERSON

I want to be the best I can be.

I know what to do. I do my chores.

I do what I am told and what is right because I am obedient and respectful.

I am a responsible person.

I listen and pay attention.

I stay on task and finish my work. I am loyal and faithful

To my family, school, and country.

I am a responsible person.

I keep up with my daily work
and fulfill my promises.

I use my time wisely and finish all my assignments.

PROVERBS ARE THE JOURNEY OF LIFE

I am a responsible person.

I am proud of my achievements.
I always strive to be successful and learn what I don't know.

I do my homework on time.
I study for my exams and stay away from things that are bad for me.

I am a responsible person.

I am honorable and truthful.
I don't lie or cheat.

I give my friends a hand when they need me.
I help when there is hurt.

JOHN A. SHALHOUB

I am always motivated, determined,
•and anxious to be the best I can be in character,
achievement, and personality.

PROVERBS ARE THE JOURNEY OF LIFE

I CARE, YOU CARE

I CARE, YOU CARE

JOHN A. SHALHOUB

I CARE, YOU CARE

I care about you; you care about me; I need you, and you need me.

We all care about each other.

I care about my grades.
I care about my school.
I care about my teacher.
I care about my family.

I care when you're hurt and when you have a problem.

I care when you're sad, and I am glad when you're glad.

I care when you're unhappy, and I care when you are in stress.

I care about my attitude and about my manners.

PROVERBS ARE THE JOURNEY OF LIFE

I care about how you feel about me and I about you.

I care about your feelings and how you care about mine.

I respect how you feel about me, and I about you.
Let us be honest, kind, and gentle.

Respect, I want you to give me, and respect I want to give you.

Let us be honest, kind, and friendly.
Both of us have integrity.

JOHN A. SHALHOUB

I SHARE, YOU SHARE, WE SHARE!

I SHARE, YOU SHARE, WE SHARE!

PROVERBS ARE THE JOURNEY OF LIFE

I SHARE, YOU SHARE, WE SHARE

I share, you share. We both share.
We share respect; we share kindness.

I share, you share. We both share. We share love.
We share integrity.

I share, you share. We both share.
We share friendship. We share caring.

I share, you share. We both share. We share
honesty; we share truth.

I share, you share. We both share.
We share compassion; we share love.

I share, you share. We both share. We share work;
we share support.

We share loyalty. We share values.

We both share.

We share kindness and respect,

JOHN A. SHALHOUB

We share love and understanding.

We are both friends and need each other so we can live in a peaceful world.

Sharing is a gift of love,
And faith do let us
Share and be happy.

PROVERBS ARE THE JOURNEY OF LIFE

INTEGRITY

INTEGRITY

JOHN A. SHALHOUB

INTEGRITY

I am kind, fair, and truthful.

I am honest, reliable, and dependable.

I do my work, finish my assignments, and am proud of my work.
I am obedient, and I listen and follow directions.

I am disciplined and organized, and I use my time wisely.

I am neat, clean, and dressed right.

I am friendly, respectful, and helpful.

I am ambitious, motivated, and determined to do my work.
I have a vision.
I use my mind and seek advice when I need it.

PROVERBS ARE THE JOURNEY OF LIFE

I set my goals.

I work hard to achieve them with diligence and care.

I am responsible and accountable.

I keep my promises.

I will succeed, I will triumph,

I will be whatever I want to be.

Integrity is honesty, honor, and respect.

JOHN A. SHALHOUB

I AM A GOOD CITIZEN

I AM A GOOD CITIZEN

PROVERBS ARE THE JOURNEY OF LIFE

I AM A GOOD CITIZEN

I am a good citizen, and you are a good citizen.
We both are good citizens.

We both care for each other.
I won't hurt you, and you won't hurt me.
I trust you and you trust me.
We both trust each other.

I need you and you need me.
Let me work with you and you with me.

I don't lie to you, and you don't lie to me.
We both need each other.

I don't cheat; you don't cheat; we both are honest.

I am trustworthy; you are trustworthy; we both have integrity.

JOHN A. SHALHOUB

You are fair; I am fair; we both are fair to each other.

I am loyal and faithful.

You are loyal and faithful.

We both are loyal and faithful to each other.

I am kind; you are kind.

Let us treat each other with kindness and respect.

We both have dignity because we are good citizens.

PROVERBS ARE THE JOURNEY OF LIFE

TODAY, WE WORK!

TODAY, WE WORK!

JOHN A. SHALHOUB

TODAY, WE WORK!

21 March 1996

1. Today, I am free of anxiety and worry. I am happy, relaxed, and cheerful.
2. Today, I am kind, gentle, and generous. I am courteous, friendly, and charming.
3. Today, I am genuine, truthful, and happy. I am tolerant, compromising, and forgiving.
4. Today, I am free of stress, anger, and moaning. I am strong, resourceful, and patient.
5. Today, I set aside the worries of the world and overflow with faith, hope, and charity.
6. Today, I am sociable, friendly, and helpful. I am in the world with laughter and a smile.
7. Today, the Lord lives in me. He gives me peace and sets me free.
8. Today, I live for tomorrow, and tomorrow is for today. I want to know you, and you to know me.
9. Come today, join me; tomorrow is today, and today is tomorrow. Let us make the best of today.

10. Life is you and me; we need to work together for a better world. Today is today!

JOHN A. SHALHOUB

THIS IS RESPECT

THIS IS RESPECT

THIS IS RESPECT

21 March 1996

1. Respect is to treat others the way you want to be treated.
2. Respect is to act nicely at home and school.
3. Respect is to be polite to people.
4. Respect is to be considerate of the feelings of others.
5. Respect is to think well of others.
6. Respect is to respect people no matter who they are.
7. Respect is not to be rude to adults, children, or animals.
8. Respect is to be kind, friendly and courteous.
9. Respect is not to be mean or nasty to others.
10. Respect is to be nice to others even when they are not.
11. Respect is to always have good manners.
12. Respect is to share with and to care for others.
13. Respect is to be kind to younger children.
14. Respect is not to be angry with others.
15. Respect is to be helpful to others when they need you.
16. Respect is to be happy and content.

17. Respect is to care for your family and friends.
18. Respect means being polite and having good manners.
19. Respect is to help your family and friends.
20. Respect makes you feel happy inside when you do well.
21. Respect makes you love everybody.
22. Respect makes you feel humble and truthful.
23. Respect builds you up and gives you self-confidence.
24. Respect is to love yourself and others.
25. Respect is to be loyal to your family and friends.

PROVERBS ARE THE JOURNEY OF LIFE

KEEP YOUR PROMISE

KEEP YOUR PROMISE

KEEP YOUR PROMISE

May 13, 2024

Boston, Massachusetts

- Keep your promises and remain steadfast; let your integrity guide you and never falter.

- Be someone others can rely on, a beacon of trust and dependability.

- Ask the right questions and take responsibility for the answers you provide.

- Avoid making assumptions, and never doubt the accuracy of answers without thorough research and collaboration.

- Approach life with enthusiasm—reject laziness.

- Remember, laziness leads to the brink of poverty, while ambition belongs to those who persevere, even when the road becomes difficult.

- Honorable people uphold honesty and refuse to be defeated by failure.

PROVERBS ARE THE JOURNEY OF LIFE

- True kindness shines through humility and love—it is seen in the way we treat others with respect.

- Those with vision are the creators and innovators.

- Their achievements inspire us, offering examples of what's possible through determination and creativity.

- Ground your expectations, not your imagination, without evidence.

- Life may spiral out of control at times but do not give up. Press on with courage in the relentless pursuit of solutions.

JOHN A. SHALHOUB

HOW TO FACE LIFE

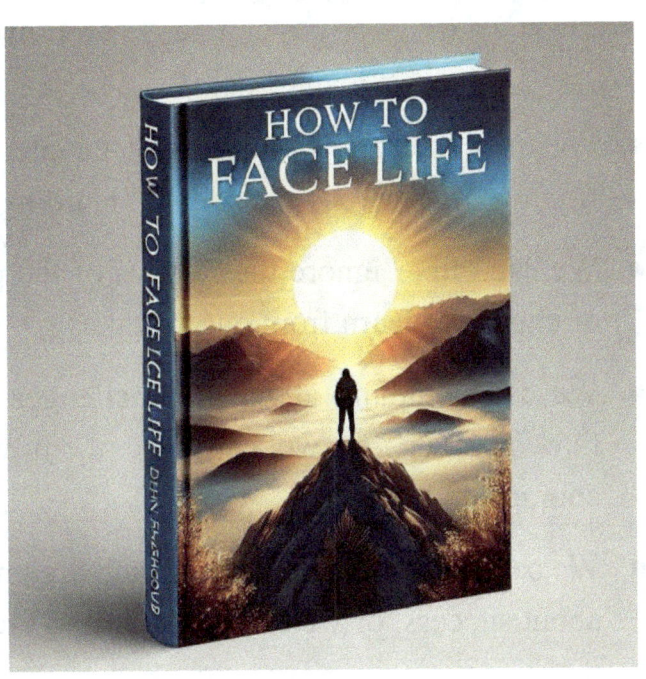

HOW TO FACE LIFE

HOW TO FACE LIFE
11 October 2011

- We may aspire to be leaders of people, but first, we must become leaders of learning.

- We can either ignore the failures of the past or choose to learn from our mistakes.

- We can complain about the challenges life throws at us, or we can face them with courage and resolve.

- We can spend our time talking and dreaming about success, or we can work hard to create it.

- If we want our children to learn, think, and read, we must lead by example—showing them how to embrace new information and turn it into actionable plans.

- If we want our children to be brave and resourceful, we must teach them to take risks, explore new ideas, and find innovative ways to solve problems.

- If we want our children to be loyal, patriotic, and responsible, we must show them the value of staying true to their goals and commitments.

- If we desire new and better schools, we must strive to be honest, dedicated educators. Only by seeking the best for us and our communities can we achieve the good and happy life we all hope for.

PROVERBS ARE THE JOURNEY OF LIFE

NOW I KNOW MY ALPHABET

NOW I KNOW MY ALPHABET

JOHN A. SHALHOUB

NOW I KNOW MY ALPHABET

21 March 1996

- Approach your goals with vigor.

- Be kind to others and honest with yourself.

- Concentrate on your work; finish what you begin.

- Depend on yourself to achieve your dreams.

- Endure hardships, for they bear the fruits of labor.

- Face challenges with pride, not defeat with shame.

- Give your best so you live without regrets.

- Help others, asking nothing in return.

- Imagine yourself atop a hill where others look to you for guidance.

- Judge no one and ignore no one.

- Know yourself, for self-awareness leads to triumph, even when all seems hopeless.

PROVERBS ARE THE JOURNEY OF LIFE

- Love your family, and let go of hatred.

- Master a skill, and you will never go hungry. However, neglecting learning and poverty may follow.

- Navigate life's minefields with care—a single misstep can change everything.

- Observe Mother Nature; she teaches wisdom and skill.

- Pardon those who harm you, and peace will dwell within your soul.

- Quit bad habits, examine your thoughts, and avoid the company of those who plot evil.

- Read instructions, follow directions, and trust your heart when doubt arises.

- Stop to lend a hand to those in need; one day, they may return the favor.

- Teach what you know, and others will be grateful.

- An ugly spirit tarnishes even the most beautiful soul.

- Visit your neighbor and befriend them—one day, you may need their kindness.

- Wage war against evil.

- X out temptation and follow the path of goodness all your days.

- You are the master of your destiny, the captain of your soul.

- Zero in on your needs with humility and fulfill them with gratitude.

PROVERBS ARE THE JOURNEY OF LIFE

COURAGE IS WHAT WE NEED

28 November 2024

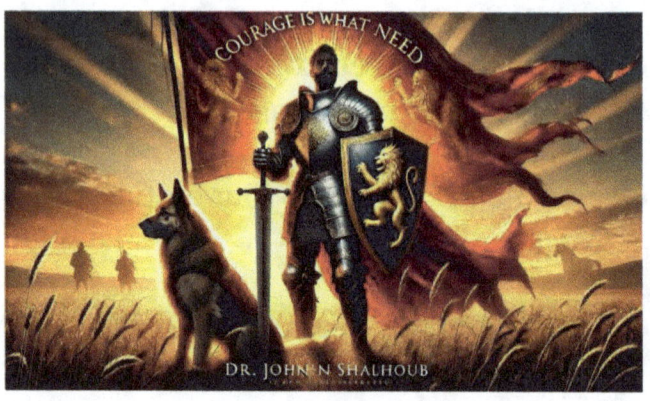

COURAGE IS WHAT WE NEED

JOHN A. SHALHOUB

COURAGE IS WHAT WE NEED

18 November 2024

- Courage is what we need to navigate life's challenges and to stand firm on our feet.

- Loyalty keeps our friends close, ensuring we are surrounded by people we trust in times of need.

- Honest friends are treasures; they can be trusted and provide the safety and support every soul craves.

- Truth is the infinite wisdom of life. It is what leads us to everlasting peace, free from worry and fear.

- We are mirrors of life for our souls, and our souls reflect the essence of existence—bridging the past, present, and future.

- Kindness soothes our hearts, offering comfort in moments of grief and sadness.

- Those who cannot speak the truth cannot be honest or offer comfort to others. Without truth, they fail to embody the essence of a truly happy human being.

- To be genuinely good, we must believe in truth and extend our hands to those in need.

- We are but travelers in this world. As we came, so shall we go—journeying along a one-way path.

- Let us remember no one escapes the consequences of their actions, whether good or bad.

- Those who think they can evade God's judgment deceive only themselves.

- The true joy of life lies in seeking peace, forgiveness, and compassion.

- And those who seek truth will find it.

- God will reward those who refrain from harming others.

JOHN A. SHALHOUB

LIFE MANAGEMENT

LIFE MANAGEMENT

PROVERBS ARE THE JOURNEY OF LIFE

LIFE MANAGEMENT
February 2, 2024

1. Character and good work are the foundation of success.

2. Honest work, vision, motivation, inspiration, hard work, focus, persistence, achievement, and victory.

3. Do not meet ignorance with ignorance, for that is precisely what ignorance seeks: to take control of the situation.

4. Prejudice, bigotry, and foolishness corrode both the mind and the heart.

5. Do not look down on others and avoid arrogance.

6. Those who lie and deceive will eventually drown in the cesspool of their own falsehood and foolishness.

7. The self-righteous, self-worshiping, and insincere will not see the face of God, for He will disown them.

8. Those who deceive others will be deceived in turn, and their days will be few.

PROVERBS ARE THE JOURNEY OF LIFE

LIFE MANAGEMENT IS A MOTTO FOR A BETTER LIFE!

LIFE MANAGEMENT IS A MOTTO FOR A BETTER LIFE!

JOHN A. SHALHOUB

THE AUTHOR

ABOUT THE AUTHOR:

Background of Reverend John A. Shalhoub

Personal Background:

Reverend John A. Shalhoub was born on February 25, 1943, in Aitha El-Foukhar, Lebanon, to Andraos Ferris Shalhoub and Nour Yousef Habib. He studied at the Balamand Seminary in Lebanon from 1958 to 1964, later working in the Assyia Schools in Damascus, Syria. He immigrated to the United States on November 5, 1966, where he pursued higher education and ministry.

Ministry and Service:

Reverend Shalhoub was ordained as an Antiochian Orthodox priest on February 23, 1969, by Archbishop Michael Shaheen. He served at St. George Orthodox Church in South Glens Falls, NY (1969–1975) and later at St. Catherine Orthodox Church in Glens Falls, NY (1975–1982). He also served as an Eastern Orthodox Navy Chaplain, reaching the rank of Lieutenant Commander.

Professional Career:

Since 1985, Reverend Shalhoub has worked as an educator and counselor in Jacksonville, North Carolina, providing services to the Onslow County School System. In 1990, he founded Shalhoub

Family Counseling Services, offering psychotherapy, and family and school counseling. His writings appear regularly in the Daily News of Jacksonville, North Carolina.

Education:

- Counseling: East Carolina University (1992)
- Doctoral Studies: Fuller Theological Seminary, Pasadena, CA (1984)
- Graduate Studies in Psychology: Plattsburgh University College, NY (1971)
- Educational Psychology: St. Rose College, Albany, NY (1972)
- Undergraduate: University of Toledo (1966–1968), Siena College (1970), Adirondack Community College (1969)
- Religious Education: Balamand Seminary, Lebanon (1958–1964)

Licenses and Certifications:

- Licensed Guidance Counselor (North Carolina, 1992)
- Certified English and Social Studies Teacher (NY, 1977; NC, 1985)
- National Certified Counselor (1990)

- Licensed Professional Counselor (NC, 1990)
- Ordained Antiochian Orthodox Priest (1969)
- Commissioned U.S. Navy Chaplain (1982)

Professional Affiliations:

Reverend Shalhoub is a member of several organizations, including:

- National Education Association
- North Carolina Association of Educators
- American Counseling Association
- American Mental Health Association
- Adlerian Psychological Society

Family:

He is married to Awatif Mitri Ghareeb, and they have three sons: George Joseph, Michael Paul, and Samuel David. He also has three brothers (George, Elias, and Joseph) and two sisters (Rose and Mary).

JOHN A. SHALHOUB

DR. FR. SHALHOUB LISTENING TO A CLIENT!

DR. FR. SHALHOUB LISTENING TO A CLIENT!

ACKNOWLEDGEMENT

I am grateful for the opportunity of life and the education of the young minds that opened the door for me to write this book "Proverbs Are the Journey of Life."

It is time to honor and express deep gratitude to two extraordinary individuals whose sacrifices and resilience deserve eternal recognition, now resting in the grace and comfort of the Lord. Their lives were filled with challenges, yet their legacy remains a testament to unwavering dedication and love.

My mother, Nour, was the embodiment of hard work and perseverance. Day after day, she toiled in the fields, harvesting wheat, barley, lentils, and other crops. Her labor extended to the vineyards, where she picked grapes, mulberries, cherries, and more, never ceasing in her efforts to provide for her family.

My father, Andraos, endured immense hardship when he migrated to Brazil. Arriving in a foreign land without a word of the language or a penny to his name, he faced a life of relentless struggle. Sadly, he passed away from a heart attack at the young age of 46 when I was just eight years old.

Despite the challenges, he worked tirelessly as a peddler, carrying clothes on his back and knocking on doors to make a living. His journey was one of courage and determination, navigating life without friends or support. After his passing, my sister Rose stepped into a vital role, raising our family with strength and selflessness. Their sacrifices are etched in my diary and writings, where their legacy continues to inspire us.

Life's trials have often brought me into conflict and disagreement, yet these experiences have shaped me in profound ways. I owe a great debt of gratitude to those who guided me during my time at the Balamand Seminary. To the thrice-blessed Ignatius Hazim, the Thrice-Blessed Patriarch Theodosius Abou Rejeili, the Thrice-Blessed Bishop Elias Najim of St. Elias Shouwayya, and the Thrice-Blessed Metropolitan Archbishop Michael of Toledo, Ohio: My unwavering faith and wisdom were guiding lights that allowed me to become who I am today. For this, I am forever grateful.

I am grateful and thankful to my uncle George Shalhoup of Charleston, WVA, who helped me to come to the USA.

Lastly, I extend heartfelt thanks to the countless writers, educators, and teachers across the ages. Their wisdom and ideas have illuminated my journey through time and space, serving as a continual source of inspiration and growth.

To all these remarkable individuals, past and present, I offer my deepest gratitude.

BOOKS BY THE AUTHOR

1. The Church I Love
2. The Antiochian Orthodox Church in Structural Setting
3. Tyranny and Apathy in the Orthodox Church
4. Tears of Agony
5. The Triumph of Tears
6. This Vale of Tears
7. My Voice to the Lord (4th Edition)
8. Lord, Hear My Prayer
9. Married for Better or Worse
10. Marriage Workbook: 3 Volumes from A to Z
11. See the Fall of the Ungodly
12. The True Story of the Merger of the Antiochian Orthodox Archdioceses
13. Character from A to Z
14. What Is Impossible for Man Is Possible for God
15. Antioch Is the Journey of Life
16. Proverbs Are the Journey of Life

17. Parables Are the Way of Life

18. The Art of Growing Up

19. Our Angel to Heaven

PROVERBS ARE THE JOURNEY OF LIFE

VISION OF LIFE

VISION OF LIFE

JOHN A. SHALHOUB

CYCLE OF LIFE

CYCLE OF LIFE

PROVERBS ARE THE JOURNEY OF LIFE

JOURNEY OF LIFE

JOURNEY OF LIFE

JOHN A. SHALHOUB

JOURNEY OF LIFE

JOURNEY OF LIFE

www.ingramcontent.com/pod-product-compliance
Lightning Source LLC
Chambersburg PA
CBHW071430300426
44114CB00013B/1373